Edwin A. Sherman

New Edition of the Brief History of the Ancient and Accepted Scottish Rite of Freemasonry

together with a historic sketch of the so-called revival of Freemasonry in

1717, and other interesting and instructive matter

Edwin A. Sherman

New Edition of the Brief History of the Ancient and Accepted Scottish Rite of Freemasonry
together with a historic sketch of the so-called revival of Freemasonry in 1717, and other interesting and instructive matter

ISBN/EAN: 9783337276591

Printed in Europe, USA, Canada, Australia, Japan

Cover: Foto ©Andreas Hilbeck / pixelio.de

More available books at **www.hansebooks.com**

NEW EDITION

OF THE

BRIEF· HISTORY

OF THE

ANCIENT AND ACCEPTED SCOTTISH RITE

OF

FREEMASONRY

TOGETHER WITH A

HISTORIC SKETCH OF THE SO-CALLED REVIVAL OF FREEMASONRY IN 1717,

AND OTHER INTERESTING AND INSTRUCTIVE MATTER.

For the Information of Master Masons in General
and of Brethren of the Ancient and
Accepted Scottish Rite of Freemasonry in Particular.

Compiled from the Most Reliable Sources and from the Most
Distinguished Historians and Authors Extant, by

EDWIN A. SHERMAN, 33°,

Honorary Member of the Supreme Council for the Southern Jurisdiction
of the United States; Grand Keeper of the Seals and Archives of
the Grand Consistory of California ; Wise Master of Gethsemane
Chapter of Rose Croix, No. 5, Oakland, California , Secretary of the Masonic Veteran Association of the Pacific
Coast; Vice-President of the National Convention of Masonic Veteran Associations of
the United States, Etc., Etc., Etc.

OAKLAND, CALIFORNIA,
CARRUTH & CARRUTH, PRINTERS, 520 15TH ST,
June 24, 1890.

TO

THE MEMORY OF

MY TRUE FRIEND AND BROTHER,

THE KIND AND COURTEOUS GENTLEMAN, THE LEARNED AUTHOR, THE
PROFOUND SCHOLAR, THE DISTINGUISHED MASON, AND THE LAW-
GIVER TO THE "ANCIENT AND HONORABLE FRATER-
NITY OF FREE AND ACCEPTED MASONS,"

Albert Gailatin Mackey, 33°,

LATE SECRETARY GENERAL AND DEAN OF THE SUPREME COUNCIL OF THE
33D DEGREE OF THE "ANCIENT AND ACCEPTED SCOTTISH RITE OF
FREEMASONRY" FOR THE SOUTHERN JURISDICTION OF THE
UNITED STATES, PAST GENERAL GRAND HIGH PRIEST,
ETC., ETC., THIS LITTLE WORK IS MOST
FRATERNALLY AND AFFECTION-
ATELY DEDICATED,

By EDWIN A. SHERMAN, 33°,

THE COMPILER.

OAKLAND, CALIFORNIA,
St. John the Baptist's Day,
June 24th, 1890.

PREFACE.

In presenting this "New Edition of a Brief History of the Ancient and Accepted Scottish Rite of Freemasonry" to his Brethren of the Craft, a few prefatory remarks the Author deems to be necessary at this time.

The first edition prepared by him was under the auspices of the Grand Consistory of the State of California in the month of July, 1885, at which time he was its Deputy and Grand Lecturer as also the Deputy of Ill. Bro. Charles F. Brown, 33°, one of the Active Inspectors-General for this State. Some fifteen hundred copies were then printed and distributed gratuitously among the Brethren of the A. & A. S. Rite in particular, and the Blue Lodges throughout the State of California in general, the Grand Consistory afterwards paying for the printing and the postage cost of distribution, but no compensation was made to the writer for the compiling of the work, which had been prepared after a great deal of time expended in reading and condensing of the history of the Rite for the object had in view. Being printed only in pamphlet form, the most of the first edition was soon lost and destroyed.

Many of the Brethren having manifested their desire to have the same reproduced, the writer had already undertaken the task and it was well under way, when he was written to by the agent of publishers in the East, and solicited to prepare a portion of a new and large Masonic work of a more general and comprehensive character, which will soon make its appearance.

In that work, will appear an abridged portion of this, and of the first edition issued in July 1885, which the writer has supplied to those publishers for that work, *but not exclusively*, he retaining the original production prepared by him in 1885, as also the present work enlarged and expanded with notes and additional matter, which the limited space allotted in the forthcoming publication by the Eastern publishers would not admit.

He, however, would most cordially commend the work referred to, which is "The History of Freemasonry and Concordant Orders" to be published by L. C. Hascall & Company, publishers, New York and Boston, U. S. A., and which every Master Mason, Royal Arch Companion, Knight Templar and Scottish Rite Mason ought to have, and it should be found in every Masonic Library as it will be the best Masonic work of interest of the Century, as a general compendium of the history of our Ancient and Honorable Order.

This "New Edition of the Brief History of the Ancient and Accepted Scottish Rite of Freemasonry, etc., herewith presented, is intended more as a hand-book for reference as an epitome of history, instead of a great work. Of the abridged portion of this production, which will be published in the greater work, the reviewing editor, one of the brightest scholars of New England, Bro. H. L. Stillson, K. T., of Bennington, Vermont, says :

"My verdict of it is, that it is able, candid, intensely interesting, and a valuable contribution. You know I predicted that it would be your crowning effort for the Craft, and it is.   *   *   *   *

*   *   *   "I wonder how you managed to comprehend so much of the world's history in so short a space. There is nothing like your production in the language, and allow me to say, that I like your treatment of the English Reformation, the Protectorate, etc., better than any outline of it I have ever read. You may take this as a very great compliment, because I am no admirer of the religious views of either Oliver Cromwell or John Knox, but I can see and appreciate fairness in a historical writer as distinguished as yourself. Some standard historians' names would have descended to posterity with greater fame, had they approached you in this characteristic.

"Hughan's "Royal Order" which follows your "Scottish Rite" and is numbered chapters IV. and V. in connection with it, are splendidly written and the two will make a Masonic History of themselves."

After such a flattering encomium of the abridged portion of this work to be embraced in the greater History referred to, the writer feels confident that this production will be duly appreciated by the Brethren who may read it, yet at the same time he urgently recommends and hopes that after reading this, they will subscribe for and procure the greater work of " THE HISTORY OF FREEMASONRY AND CONCORDANT ORDERS " of which this may be said to be the "fore-runner" of the "one that cometh after it which is to be preferred before it," the clasps of which he is hardly "worthy to unloose," where there are so many more distinguished writers than himself engaged upon it, who have been reared in the classic shades of Oxford, Harvard, Yale and other colleges, while the writer has spent more than forty years of his life upon the frontiers and among the mountains and slopes of the Pacific Coast. Such as it is, however, he commits it to the destiny that awaits it, and patiently but confidently bides the result.

EDWIN A. SHERMAN, 33°.

OAKLAND, CALIFORNIA, July 1, 1890.

INTRODUCTION.

"He that is first in his own cause seemeth just; but his neighbor cometh and searcheth him."—*Prov.*

"Some things thou shalt *hele* (conceal) and some thou shalt publish and declare."—*Esdras.*

"No greater honor could accrue to any man than that of having been the founder of a new school of Masonic history, in which the fictions and loose statements of former writers would be rejected, and in which the rule would be adopted that has been laid down as a vital maxim of all inductive science,—in words that have been chosen as his motto by a recent powerful investigator of historical truth: 'Not to exceed and not to fall short of facts—not to add and not to take away. To state the truth, the whole truth, and nothing but the truth.' "—*Albert G. Mackey.*

When so much has been written and in a controversial manner by distinguished Masonic writers and varied opinions expressed by them as if *ex cathedra*, that statements, conflicting as they may be, are supposed to be taken as positive facts, infallible and certain, it may be considered rash and imprudent for another, but unpretentious writer, to enter the field and, without controversial argument, attempt to give a sketch of a Rite of Freemasonry for the benefit of the earnest seeker after Masonic truth, which Rite is the most universal and deservedly the most popular and meritorious of all the systems of Freemasonry now practiced upon the face of the globe—that of the "Ancient and Accepted Scottish Rite of Freemasonry," under the regularly constituted Supreme Councils of the World.

Says Nicholas de Bonneville: "The difficulties attendant upon writing a history of Freemasonry, to compose such a work, supported by dates and authentic facts, it would require a period equal to ten times the age of man." This statement, though an exaggerated one, contains a very large percentage of truth when we consider the age in which he lived (during the latter part of the eighteenth century), in which there were more than a hundred rites and orders of Freemasonry, and the number of degrees was legion, in which the various authors and compilers made free use of each other's inventions and productions in compiling their own; making alterations and changing the names of degrees (which was afterward followed to some extent in America), and as their rituals were both written and printed, without a copyright law for protection, while *per se* they were unable to protect their productions from infringement and being purloined bodily by their rival authors and competitors and confusion being worse confounded by the Jesuits, who sowed tares among them all.

It is a difficult matter for the ordinary American Freemason to understand or comprehend such a state of apparent confusion among the workmen, and of so much dust arising in cleaning out the rubbish and endeavoring to bring order out of chaos in the efforts made to restore the Temple to its pristine glory and splendor.   And comparisons, however odious, are necessary to be made to understand intelligently the status and difference of condition between American and European Freemasonry before entering upon this work.   Says Oliver: "The Americans appear to be more generally versed in the principles of the Order than the brethren of this country (*i. e.* Great Britain), which is owing, I conceive, to the genial operation of its local Grand Lodges. *Every brother may become a ruler of the Craft, and a Master in Israel, by his own meritorious exertions.*   The offices of the Grand Lodge are open to the industrious and worthy brethren who have given proof of their excellence in the art; and this facility of promotion excites a spirit of friendly emulation, which operates favorably for society at large.   The several Grand Lodges also are engaged in amicable contests, which shall carry out the best interests of Masonry most effectually; and hence we find nothing in Masonry as it is practiced there to condemn, but everything to commend.   They do not waste their time in talking, debates upon all speculative questions being left to the several committees or boards.   The Grand Lodges have to determine merely upon their reports, which are usually found to be drawn up with so much judgment and discrimination as not to be susceptible of any hostile opinion, and hence their members are seldom in collision with each other."

In Europe they go upon the monarchial principles and ideas expressed in Ecclesiasticus, which happily in America are not canonical:

"The wisdom of a learned man cometh by opportunity of leisure; and he that hath little business shall become wise.

"How can he get wisdom that holdeth the plough and that glorieth in the goad that driveth oxen, and is occupied in their labors and whose talk is of bullocks?

"He giveth his mind to make furrows; and is diligent to give the kine fodder.

"So every carpenter and workmaster * * * All these trust to their hands and every one is wise in his work.

"Without these cannot a city be inhabited, and they shall not dwell where they will, nor go up and down;

"They shall not be sought for in public counsel, nor sit high in the congregation; they shall not sit on the judge's seat nor understand the sentence of judgment; they cannot declare justice and judgment; and they shall not be found where parables are spoken. But they will maintain the state of the world, and all their desire is in the work of their craft."

The American Freemason stands on the broad level and solid foundation of equality and common citizenship of an absolutely free government of a democratic republic, founded by his fathers in the Revolution of more than a century ago; which has come to him as a priceless legacy by inheritance, with no law of *primo geniture* solely for the benefit of elder sons; and his natural rights by birth and citizenship are protected by constitutional laws, which, as a man truly free born in every sense, make him the equal of a king, while in Europe, from whence nearly all our Freemasonry has been originally transplanted, the European-born and created Craftsman cannot experience and feel that thrill of conscious manhood and equality at home which inspires and gives that freedom of action, of unobsequious and fearless independence of character and tone, which distinguishes his American brother without arrogance or superciliousness.

In England, Scotland and Ireland, from whence we derive our Masonic descent, there is the superincumbent mass of legally stratified and arbitrary civil and social pressure *of not less than sixty-six divisions or layers*, one above the other, of rank of royalty, blooded and created nobility and aristocracy, consisting in the male line of king, dukes, marquises, earls, viscounts, barons, baronets, knighthood, etc., etc., etc., down to and including gentlemen-at-arms, before the middle classes of merchants, bankers, manufacturers and the professions are reached, with the mechanic and laborer at the bottom of the scale of British humanity; while an equal if not greater weight, with ten-fold more despotic power of caste, exists upon the continent of Europe. Only in the United States of America is the dream of the European Freemason, of liberty, equality and fraternity materialized and made substantial and real; and here only, absolutely and completely, politically and Masonically speaking, is his *faith* lost in sight, his *hope* ended in fruition of equal civil and religious liberty, and only *charity* remains for him to practice among his brethren in "the household of the faithful" in particular, and toward all mankind in general, and maintain the principles of our Order. In Europe and in European colonies the Freemason is *a graded subject* according to his civic rank; in America, *a free citizen, where all are equal;* but everywhere around the globe *a brother*.

The Masonic doctrine enunciated by Thomas Jefferson in the Declaration of American Independence, "We hold these truths to be self-evident that *all men are created equal*, and that they are endowed with certain inalienable rights, among which are life, *liberty* and the pursuit of happiness," is the American Freemason's and the *true* American citizen's creed. Upon this he constructs his Masonic, moral, religious and political edifice, and the Grand Lodge under whose particular jurisdiction he may reside lays the corner-stones of all public buildings erected by the government of his choice, and in which he has a vote and voice.

In Europe it is but theory in part, and Freemasonry lives under the baleful shadow of united altar and throne. In America it is in both theory and practice, unrestrained, and lives and thrives under the broad sunshine of well-regulated liberty and under the "starry-decked heavens" which cover a free republic; "a government of the people, by the people and for the people," so well described by the immortal Lincoln, and said by another, "And the will of the people is the law of the land."

The social and political conditions of America and Europe are unequal, and Freemasonry in Europe, by its degrees, was, and has been for a century and three-quarters, graded according to civic rank and degree of aristocracy, and it will in all probability continue to be so for many years to come, notwithstanding the strenuous, erratic and extraordinary efforts of our French brethren, who are too iconoclastic at times, and who endeavor to remove and obliterate too many of the ancient landmarks.

Therefore, it is, that when American writers upon the subject of Freemasonry enter upon the discussion, research and history fall into the common error of traveling in old ruts made by others, like a procession of pissants, and run everything into the ground, and into as great a darkness and obscurity as existed before they started out on their expedition, and considering Freemasonry in the abstract without regard to the civic and social rank and condition of affairs in the Old World; and each, in letting out the string of his kite to cross the Atlantic, to have something attached to the bobs of its tail, gets it entantangled abroad or it becomes too heavy to again rise, and in pulling it in finds that he has miscalculated the distance, by using Mercator's projection for his trestleboard, and not allowed for the spherical form of the earth; and his kite becomes a net with the bobs for sinkers, and he finds at last that he has actually been engaged in deep-sea soundings and gathering shrimps in the Atlantic instead of bringing down illumination from the stars of an European sky.

Some of them might have learned a lesson from our own illustrious Masonic exemplar and philosopher, Benjamin Franklin, who, before he ventured upon the shores of the Old World to lecture upon the science of electricity, saw fit to test the truth of his reasoning and philosophy by tapping the battery in the clouds immediately over his head at the risk of burning his fingers and receiving a shock of enlightenment such as is not usually given in the prescribed formalities of the Craft.

When the cord was loosened or cut in Europe that bound Operative and Speculative Freemasonry together, and a division of copartnership property took place, the Speculative portion retained the working tools as *symbols only* to illustrate and inculcate moral truths; and though in the Master's Degree the candidate was informed that he was "entitled to the knowledge and use of *all* the instruments and working tools indiscriminately," "*but more especially the trowel,*" which has a beautiful moral connected with its use, and in America has its appropriate signification, yet in Europe its real meaning is adroitly and covertly concealed. If the brother should significantly attempt to make use of the drawing intruments by which symbolically he should attempt to alter or improve the plan of architecture of social and civic rank and seek to rise above his station in life, the condition of his birth and education, he would very quickly receive the admonition, "*Ne sutor ultra crepidam*" ("Let not the cobbler overstep his last".) Or, in other words, he would be directed to confine himself to the trowel and mortar-board alone, and outside upon the walls of the Temple, and not attempt anything in the way of ornament or elegance within, which belongs only to his superiors by circumstance of birth and degree of condition. It would be implied by manner, if not actually spoken, "We, who are your superiors, can for a few brief moments condescend to come down to your level; but you must not presume to ascend to ours, for, if you do, you had better emigrate."

That is the actual difference of the status between an American and an European Freemason—has ever been, is now, and will continue to be until Europe overturns these layers of stratified royalty, nobility and aristocracy, where liberty is bayoneted to the cross, and the crown with the tiara or mitre have been riveted together in the union of the Church and State.

There is a secret tradition that King Solomon had got tired of the architect of the Temple, who was the representative of the people, and who had risen from their level to become the companion of kings. The necessity of personal intercourse during the construction of the Temple had made his architect familiar with that royalty which was but recent and in the second generation only; and the Tyrian architect regarded Solomon as but a man and the son of a shepherd who, by a chain of fortuitous circumstances, had succeeded the first occupants of the throne upon the change of the autonomy and form of government of the people of Israel.

King Solomon, being jealous of his power and glory, and determined that no other monarch should erect a similar temple of equal magnificence and splendor, is said to have himself, secretly and surreptitiously, secured the plans and the last designs drawn upon the trestle-board of the Temple and secretly contrived the plot whereby his chief architect might be removed, that no other king or nation should be able to secure his services; while his grief and indignation were simulated and hypocritical, and the unconscious instruments of his purpose performed the part they were incited to enact, not knowing who was the actual chief conspirator whose will they had carried out, when they supposed that they were only executing their own, and yet received the decision of their fate at his hands, the chief criminal and conspirator acting as their judge, from whose royal decree there was no appeal. Be the tradition true or false, yet in European Freemasonry the same spirit to a certain extent still prevails, and there are not a few in America at the present time but who have imbibed the same.

While American Freemasonry retains the form, in a modified degree, of that of its progenitors, and fraternal intercourse everywhere necessarily exists under restrictions, yet its spirit and teachings are those which are best adapted to a free people, where each individual is the equal and peer of his fellows in the freedom and integrity of manhood and with equal rights, honors, privileges, duties and responsibilities of brotherhood and citizenship; and any rite of Freemasonry, order or society of any kind which has been heretofore, or hereafter may be transplanted from European to American soil that does not in due time, and after a fair trial, conform to American principles of free self-government by its adherents must, as it ought to do, cease to have an existence on this side of the Atlantic.

In this spirit of the teachings of true Freemasonry, stripped of its surplusage, the writer approaches the task before him, to be found in the following chapters, and if a thorough experience of thirty-six years of a Masonic life (twenty-three of which have been officially spent in the Ancient and Accepted Scottish Rite), of careful study, research, and intercourse with not a few of the wisest and best, who have been, and some still living are, ornaments to the Fraternity, who have illuminated the pages of the history of their country and of Freemasonry, has not taught him anything of value that he may impart to his "Brethren of the Mystic Tie," then has his whole Masonic life been misspent and his present efforts useless and vain.

As the bee-hive, in a healthy condition, without drones or moths to eat out and destroy its substance, represents a well-regulated and well-governed Lodge and each individual a worker-bee, armed for its own defense and of its hive, goes forth to its unlimited field of labor independent and free, gathers the pollen and nectar of flowers for the sustenance of itself and its fellows, and all working to the same common purpose and end; so the writer, like the bee whether gathering from the roses and daisies of England, the thistles and heather of Scotland, the willows of Germany, the lillies of France, or the honey-dew of America, which everywhere abounds, endeavor to contribute something of the fruit of his labors to the common stock, carefully avoiding the poison of dogwood blooms, the distillation of deadly nightshade and noxious vegetation which might be injurious to his fellows and make unhealthy the condition of the Masonic hive.

Fraternally yours,

OAKLAND, CALIFORNIA,   EDWIN A. SHERMAN, 33°.
St. John the Baptist's Day,
    June 24th, 1890.

CHAPTER I.

THE CONTEMPORANEOUS HISTORY CO-EVAL WITH THE DAWN
AND RISE OF SPECULATIVE OR PHILOSOPHICAL
FREEMASONRY IN EUROPE.

"The Grand Kabalistic Association known in Europe under the name of
"FREEMASONRY" appeared all at once in the world at the period when the
Protest against the Papal Power came to break the Christian unity." The
destruction of the Order of Knights Templar and the burning at the stake of
Jacques De Molay, their last Grand Master, in Paris, on the 11th of March,
1313, with thousands of others proscribed or persecuted to their death under
the pretext of heresy, and who were excommunicated and scattered under the
terrible conspiracy of Pope Clement V., Philip the Fair of France and the
ultramontane Order of Knights of St. John of Jerusalem, who received as a
reward for their perfidy the possessions of the Templars in the islands of
Rhodes and of Malta (and receiving a new title, that of the "Knights of
Malta"), caused the remnants of Knights Templars to seek refuge in other
countries than their own, where they might enjoy " life, liberty and the pursuit of happiness."

One portion fled to Germany, where they found protection under an
excommunicated Emperor, who incorporated them into a branch of the
Teutonic Order of Knights of St. Mary, who had fought by their side against
the Saracens under Saladin in the wars of the Crusades. Their *beauseant,* or
battle-flag, of black and white in the form of a pennon (or swallow tail),
which they could no longer carry, was taken from them, the swallow-tail part
cut off, and that they might always be able to see their colors and to remind
them of the blood of the martyred Templars, so unjustly and wickedly put to
death, the broad red stripe was placed under it and adopted as the flag of
Germany, which still continues to be the standard of that nation to-day under
the house of Brandenburg.

Being no longer bound by the vows of a military priesthood and of
chastity in Germany, some of them contracted matrimonial alliances with
their own country women; yet, to distinguish their origin and maintain a
distinct organization within themselves and that their wrongs might not be
forgotten, they adopted a name after that of the founder of the Order of the
Temple, Hugo de Payens de Guenoe, which became a password among them
for their greater security, from which fact, and the origin of their Order and
distinction and condemned as heretics, they came to be more generally and
popularly known as " LES HUGUENOTS." Having preserved their blood and

language distinct they gradually returned to France, from which in after years, upon the revocation of the Edict of Nantes in 1685, they were again robbed of their property, expelled from France and driven to other countries— being a repetition of the same thing which in 1313 had been visited upon their ancestors, the Knights Templars.

The remnants of Knights Templars in England, Scotland and Ireland were ordered to dissolve their organization, disband and become incorporated with the English branch of Knights of St. John of Jerusalem (or Knights of Malta), to enter their priories and preceptories, or suffer the like consequences as had been visited upon their brethren in France and throughout Southern Europe. Edward II., the son-in-law of their bitter foe (Philip the Fair of France), was then on the throne of England, and equally fierce in his determination to carry out the relentless measures of persecution against the Templars in his dominion.

America had not then been discovered, and there was no place of refuge in the British Isles except in the Kingdom of Scotland, then harrassed by raids from England across the border and threatened with subjugation by Edward II. It was at a time when Robert the Bruce, the rightful heir to the Scottish throne, was contending for the freedom and independence of Scotland and his lawful inheritance to the crown. To him this remnant of Knights Templars fled for protection. He had led a portion of them in the wars of the Holy Land, to regain possession of the sepulchre of Christ. Their faith in him did not prove groundless, but the name of Knight Templar, as elsewhere throughout Europe, had to be dropped on account of the hostility and power of their enemies, and that branch was incorporated by Bruce into the Order of " Knights of St. Andrew of Scotland," of Chardon, or of the Thistle, which, with their aid on St. John the Baptists' Day, the 24th of June, 1314 (a little more than a year after their last Grand Master, De Molay, had been burned at the stake), at the Battle of Bannockburn the forces of Edward II. were overthrown, the independence of Scotland was secured, and Robert Bruce was restored to the throne. In honor of the victory secured by him on that day he instituted the Order of the Rosy Cross, which served alike for the Knights of St. Andrew of Scotland and the Knights Templars, who had been incorporated into that Order. That in the persecutions, suffering, death, burial, resurrection and ascension of the Saviour the Knights Templars might see symbolized the persecution, suffering and death of their Grand Master, De Molay, and the resurrection of their lost cause and restoration of their possessions wrongfully held by the Knights of Malta; while as Scottish Knights of St. Andrew they saw the past woes of Scotland, her deep misery and degradation heaped upon her by the same relentless foe, and which had now risen, with their aid, to a glorious independence, with the brightest hopes of peace, prosperity and happiness before her. An example afterward followed successfully in more modern times by the Carbonari Patriot Masons of Italy against the remorseless oppression of the Papal tyranny, and which at last, with the aid of such distinguished Masons and patriots as Garibaldi, Mazzini, Cavour and others, under Victor Emanuel, who secured the freedom and unity of Italy, with Rome for its capital, and overthrew the power of the Pope;

which condition is still continued by King Humbert at the present day, with rights of conscience enjoyed by all, and Masons and others are no longer immured in dungeons to die of starvation or be tortured by the Inquisition for having a copy of the Bible, our Great Light, in their possession.

From the loins of the old Knights Templars of Great Britain and France and Germany sprang the Fathers of Freemasonry and the Reformation; and to them is the Masonic world indebted for all that there is of Speculative Freemasonry, their colleges of science and philosophy, with the grand triune principles of Liberty, Equality and Fraternity emblazoned on its banners, with the interlaced triangles of Faith, Hope and Charity.

The subsequent wars between England and Scotland caused many to flee from Scotland to the Continent and seek asylum in France and Germany, and to again return to their native land when the times were more propitious and there were favorable opportunities. And for nearly five hundred years the chivalry of Scotland was in constant migration to and from the Continent, and it was but natural that during that long period those descended from the Knights Templars of Scotland, when seeking an asylum abroad, where they were welcomed as friends and given protection, should carefully seek out those of the same blood and visit the localities where once had stood the priories and preceptories of their Templar ancestry. In those times Scotchmen *generally traveled in foreign countries* while the English landsman remained at home.

The minstrelsy of Europe still sang the songs and related the stories and tales of the deeds of the chivalrous Crusaders, which kept up the martial spirit of the knighthood, whose powers and achievements in arms were turned in other directions, while the strides of the Reformation through streams and seas of blood and persecution for three centuries, changed the character of nearly the whole of the population of Europe and converted the Island of Great Britain into a home of refuge for the persecuted, exiled reformers, fleeing before the armies of the Papacy, led by'those bloodhounds in human form, the Dominicans and Jesuits. On the Continent of Europe Operative Freemasonry was comparatively at a halt. The renunciation of the Papal authority by Henry VIII. and declaring the English Church independent of the Vatican, and the encouragement given to the Operative Freemasons in the erection of new church edifices that were to be used for the preaching of the Gospel according to St. John the " Beloved Disciple," and not that of the so-called successor to St. Peter, added fresh fuel to the fire of the wrath of the Pope at Rome.

When Elizabeth, upon the death of " Bloody Mary," was called to the throne, both England and Scotland were in a constant state of inflammation, consequent upon the great religious conflicts and warfare which extended throughout Christendom. Under her patronage a new style of architecture was introduced, called the " *Elizabethean*," and newer designs were being drawn upon the trestle-boards by the Master Workmen of the Craft, while the noblest spirits, poets, scholars and philosophers of the age found patronage and protection at the hands of this masculine " Virgin Queen of England," against whom the thunders of the Vatican roared in vain, and the daggers of its Jesuit assassins failed when directed at the breast of their intended royal victim.

Scotland felt the impulse and force of the waves of commotion and revolution of mental and religious changes, caused by the upheaval and resistless forces of the Great Reformation, and when Elizabeth passed away on the 24th of March, 1603, and was succeeded by James VI., the Protestant King of Scotland, who became James I. of England, uniting the thrones of both countries on July 25th, 1603, in the very dawn of the seventeenth century— an age of stupendous convulsions and disturbances, which shook the British Isles to their foundations, and were the cause of forced as well as voluntary expatriations and first peopling the Atlantic shores of America with English colonies, along the watery edge of a rock-rimmed wilderness peopled with hostile savages, but where the vision of St. John the Evangelist was fully materialized in after years in the form of civil and religious liberty. "And the woman fled into the wilderness, where she hath a place prepared of God." "And to the woman were given two wings of a great eagle, that she might fly into the wilderness, into her place where she is nourished * * * from the face of the serpent."

Religious freedom in part was secured, the Scottish King of England and the United Kingdom has the "Great Light" brought forth and translated out of the dead tongues and given to the people, and read openly in the churches in a language that can be heard and all understand. He provides an honored place for it in public processions, in the coronation ceremonies, to be forever used in the crowning of the Protestant kings of Great Britain and none others, and from which in after years the same ceremonies modified are to be continually used in the installations of Master of Lodges of Freemasonry and other ceremonies of the Craft. Rome has nothing to expect in her favor from James I., and through her deadly corps of Jesuit conspirators and assassins attempts to destroy both James I. and the Parliament of England by blowing them into the air. Fortunately for him and his kingdom and humanity, the "Gunpowder Plot" fails, and the immediate conspirators and assassins meet the due punishment of their intended crime, while the Pope, in anger and disappointment, says low mass for the repose of their damned souls.

The first quarter of the century passes away, terminating his reign on the throne by a natural death, on the 27th of March, 1625, and he is succeeded by his eldest son, Charles I., but during the latter's reign, midst civil war and revolutions, having married Henrietta Marie (daughter of Henry IV. of France), a Roman Catholic wife, and imported a retinue and horde of priests and Jesuits with her from France, the realm was rent with revolution, wars and bloodshed, until at last he was brought to trial by Parliament, and two years before the first half of the century closes he is beheaded, on the 30th of January, 1648, for his treason to the British constitution and to the people.

In the midst of these wars and troubles Operative Freemasonry was inactive and silent, while Speculative Freemasonry, in connection with it, as we now have it, had not been dreamed of by the wisest of philosophers and scholars of those days. The protectorate of Cromwell, however, materially changed this state of affairs. On the pacification of the people and the restoration of peace, the affairs of Great Britain underwent a favorable transformation, and he caused her flag to be honored at home, respected abroad and dreaded by her enemies throughout the world. At home the schools and universities advanced to a high state of improvement and culture; commerce, manufactures and navigation flourished to a degree that had never been reached before; and the erection of magnificent buildings and structures had begun to a liberal extent, giving employment to architects and guild of Freemasons in their construction, when suddenly it was brought to a dead stop by the death of Cromwell on the 3d of September, 1658. The year and a half that his son Richard ruled as the Protector of the Commonwealth was not marked with any event of importance, and the tide of progress and good government was to be turned back, and all the evils which could be brought upon a nation within itself were consummated upon the accession of Charles II. to the throne on the 29th of May, 1660; and for the twenty-five years of his reign of revenge profligacy, debauchery and immorality, no period of the world's history since the days just before the flood has there been its equal among any people. If he could have covered his kingdom with a roof he would have converted it into a general house of prostitution, if he had been able to entirely debauch and corrupt the people. During his reign, in the Summer of 1664 the Great Plague broke out in London and spread over the kingdom, and in London alone, in the short space of four months, not less than one hundred thousand people were swept away by its ravages. Two years afterward, on the 3d of September, 1666, the Great Fire of London broke out, which raged for three days, in which over thirteen thousand houses and ninety churches were destroyed, including St. Paul's, which was also laid in ashes. To restore and rebuild the city caused the influx of an immense gathering of Operative Masons from all over the kingdom and from abroad to find employment in London, which also received a new addition of population from the expatriated Huguenots from France and other religious reformers, who, in exile, sought security from persecution, hoping to find that freedom of conscience denied them at home. These people having to depend upon their own industry for their maintenance fused with the guilds of London and the other cities in their various branches of labor and swelled the ranks of Operative Freemasons and other organizations, and indoctrinated them with their own ideas of religious liberty.

On the 6th day of February, 1685, the world was relieved of the presence of Charles II., and on the 23d of April following (1685) his brother, James II., ascended the throne, and the last of the male line of the Stewarts was crowned King of Great Britain and Ireland. But he, treacherous and false to his oath, after four years' efforts to restore the supremacy of the Papacy, is forced to abdicate by the people and driven into exile, from whence he returns to make one more, and the last, but fruitless effort to regain his throne.

The revocation of the Edict of Nantes by Louis XIV. of France in 1685, had driven a million of Huguenots, with their families, to England, Holland and America, and William of Nassau and Prince of Orange—the grandson of William the Silent and great-grandson of Coligny, the Huguenot Admiral of France, slain at the Massacre of St. Bartholomew—was called to the throne, with the Protestant daughter of James II. as Queen, and they were jointly crowned as William III. and Mary II., King and Queen of Great Britain, Ireland and the Colonial Dependencies.

The joy which prevailed throughout Great Britain and the American Colonies knew no bounds, and only in Ireland was there discontent and rebellion, which was speedily settled by the victory of William the Prince of Orange over the combined armies of the Papal French invaders and Irish rebels under James II., at the Battle of the Boyne, in Ireland, on the 12th of July, 1690 (or just two hundred years ago), when peace was restored throughout the entire kingdom. The augmentation of the population by the forced emigra- tion of the Huguenots from France made up the loss of those destroyed by the Great Plague, and many of them entered the army and navy, gave valuable assistance in winning the victories over the invaders and rebels in Ireland. Others, skilled in the arts and sciences, scholars and philosophers, were settled all over the kingdom; but a large proportion were domiciled in in London and the other cities of the realm.

The seeds of the Reformation sown in Scotland in the middle of the sixteenth century by John Knox, had borne abundant fruit and transformed nearly the whole people, excepting a few clans in the Highlands. In 1546, he, with his people, had entered the Castle of St. Andrews as a place of safety from the Romish clergy, but in 1547 they were compelled to surrender to the combined forces of the Roman Catholics of Scotland and France. Knox was taken a prisoner to France and forced to work as a slave in the galleys for two years, when he was released and returned to Scotland and again entered upon "his preaching with his best beloved brethren of the congregation of the Castle of St. Andrews."

The constant wars, civil and foreign combined, in Scotland, the destruc- tion of castles and fortresses as well as edifices, gave the opportunity in times of peace for the employment to the Operative Freemasons to rebuild and repair the damages and ravages of war, while the principles of civil and relig- ious liberty steadily inculcated among the people, found a secure lodgment among the brethren of the Craft, to whom the Great Light had been specially intrusted for safe keeping, which they were enabled to read by the three lesser lights, themselves a symbol of Divine truth, that, being placed in trian- gular form, produced *one light* without one candle casting a shadow upon the other (as there would be if two or more were placed in line), thus represent- ing or illustrating the doctrine of the Trinity of the Godhead or his attributes·

Upon the accession of William III. the Prince of Orange to the throne, confidence was restored throughout the kingdom, and he, recognizing the peaceful character, industry and loyalty of the Craft, whose occupation was to build, and not destroy, directed that their aprons and other ·insignia to be bordered with blue as a mark of union and fidelity, which afterward (in 1730) became a standing regulation, from which time "Ancient Craft Masonry" has been termed "Blue Masonry" and the Lodges "Blue Lodges," and are thus designated and known as such throughout the world. It is well to note in this connection that the Huguenot colors were blue and white, and blue is the color of Scotland.

It was during the latter half of the seventeenth century that the nebulæ of speculative or Philosophic Freemasonry was gradually taking the form of a solar and stellar system in conjunction with the operative, as being accepted in addition to that which it already possessed. It was during this period that the Craft was chiefly under the direction and charge of one whose name in history is, and always will be, inseparable from that of Freemasonry—Sir Christopher Wren.

"This man (the son of a rector of the Established Church) was born October 20th, 1632, in the reign of Charles I. When fourteen years of age he entered Wadham College, Oxford, as a gentleman commoner, and was even then distinguished for his mathematical knowledge and for having invented several astronomical and mathematical instruments. In 1645 he became a member of the Scientific Club connected with Gresham College, from which the Royal Society subsequently arose. In 1657 he removed permanently to London, having been elected Professor of Astronomy at Gresham College. He was not professionally an architect, but from his youth he had devoted much time to its theoretic study, and during the Parliamentary wars and the rule of the protectorate under Cromwell he kept away entirely from the contests of party. In 1660 he was appointed by Charles II. one of a commission to superintend the restoration of the Cathedral of St. Paul's, which had been much dilapidated, but before the designs could be carried out the Great Fire of London occurred, in which St. Paul's Cathedral was also reduced to ashes, and in 1665 Wren went to Paris and other cities of the continent to study the designs of the various churches and other public buildings. While assistant to Sir John Denham, the Surveyor-General, he directed his attention to the restoration of the burnt portion of the city, and in 1667 he was appointed Surveyor-General and Chief Architect, and as such he erected a large number of churches, the Royal Exchange, Greenwich Observatory and other public edifices. But his crowning work and masterpiece is the Cathedral of St. Paul, commenced in 1675 and finished in 1710; but the cap-stone was laid in 1708, at which there was a great celebration."—*Mackey.*

One writer says that "Christopher Wren was the President of the London Guild of Freemasons at the time of the Commonwealth (under the Protectorate of Oliver Cromwell); that they held their meetings secret in the Common Hall of Freemasons, and that their *real object was political*—the restoration of the monarchy—hence the necessary exclusion of the public and the oaths of secrecy enjoined on the members. The pretense of promoting architecture and the choice of the place where to hold their meetings, suggested by their President, were no more than blinds to deceive the existing government."— *C. W. King.*

Another writer says: "This day, May the 18th, being Monday, 1691, after Rogation Sunday, is a great convention at St. Paul's Church of the fraternity of the ADOPTED MASONS, where Sir Christopher Wren *is to be adopted a Brother* and Sir Henry Goodrich of the Tower, and divers others. There have been Kings that have been of this sodality."—*Aubrey.*

From these two facts it is evident that Wren, being the son of a rector of the Established Church under Charles I., was naturally opposed to the rule of Cromwell as Protector, which is confirmed by his being appointed Surveyor General by Charles II. immediately after the restoration of the Stuarts to the throne; and it is also confirmatory of the fact that the "Adopted" or

Accepted Masons, or rather Speculative and Philosophic Masons, then connected with the Operative, at that time were composed of gentlemen who were
Protestants and especially loyal to that cause which had elevated William the
Prince of Orange to the throne and had forced James II. to flee from his
kingdom.   And that until that period when peace prevailed throughout the
realm and no hope existed for the restoration of the Stuarts, that further
cause of suspicion as to Wren's loyalty to the reigning family had ceased to
exist, and therefore he was admitted to full fellowship with others, and as
both Operative and Speculative he could serve as Grand Master to and after
the completion (of the Temple) of St. Paul's Cathedral.   Certainly his visit
to Paris and elsewhere on the Continent in the service of Charles II. (who
was expected to restore the Roman Catholic religion in England) gave him
facilities of admission into churches and other buildings, where courtesies
were extended to him with the expectation that in his rebuilding of St. Paul's
Cathedral in London he would be reproducing a second St. Peter's, like that
at Rome, in which the Romish and not the Anglican service would be held.
At any rate, it is certain that in the communion of priests and laity even then
there was what is now designated as "High Church," with a very thin par-
tition between itself and Rome, and the "Low Church" party, which
adhered strictly to the tenets of the Protestant faith.   But Speculative or
Philosophic Freemasonry was then in its first stage of organization, preparing
for its grand work before it in the opening of the eighteenth century,
when all questions of philosophy and science which agitated the public mind
could be discussed and opinions expressed without danger of kingly or eccle-
siastical censure or punishment within the kingdom.   Christopher Wren had
now become too old to perform the duties of Patron or Grand Master, and as
there were no other great buildings to be constructed at that time many of the
Operative Masons dispersed, and Operative as well as Speculative Masonry
combined began to temporarily fall into decay, and in 1716 Christopher
Wren's life ended, and his tomb in the crypt of St. Paul's Cathedral was appropriately inscribed with the words, "*Si monumentum requiris, circumspice.*"
("If you desire to find his monument, look around").

But Wren had done more than merely draw designs and superintend the
construction of material edifices.   The moral lessons in connection with the
working tools, which had been enlarged under his direction and supervision,
were to be carried by the craftsmen into every part of the world where they
journeyed and found employment.   Though they were simple and crude, yet
interwoven as they were with their labors, they were the primer series of
what was to be unfolded and developed in future years by others.

CHAPTER II.

THE SO-CALLED REVIVAL OF FREEMASONRY IN 1717 AND
ITS DEVELOPMENT WITH CONCURRENT HISTORY
OF THE EIGHTEENTH CENTURY.

Upon the so-called revival of Freemasonry in 1717, when the Lodges were separate and independent of each other, and there never having been a governing Grand Lodge before, a French Huguenot Reformer, John Theophilus Desaguliers, born at Rochelle, France, March 12th, 1683, having become a curate of the Church of England and initiated in the "Lodge of Antiquity" in St. Paul's church-yard, secured the assistance of several older Masons to aid in the formation of the *first* Grand Lodge of England. He succeeded in obtaining a meeting of the four London Lodges on St. John the Baptist's Day, June 24th, 1717, when the Grand Lodge of Masons was organized at the Apple Tree Tavern, and Antony Sayer, the son of a French Huguenot, was elected the first Grand Master. In 1718 he was succeeded by George Payne, and in 1719 Desaguliers was elected Grand Master, followed by the Duke of Wharton, the Earl of Dalkeith, Lord Paisley and others.

Desaguliers was the son of a French Huguenot clergyman, who fled to England in 1685 on the revocation of the Edict of Nantes. He was more of a scientist than a preacher, and Priestly styles him "an indefatigable experimental philosopher." His frequent personal intercourse with Sir Christopher Wren, with whom he was on terms of the most intimate friendship, enabled him to greatly profit from the experience and information given by so distinguished a man.

In remodeling the work of Speculative Freemasonry, engrafted upon the Operative, the myth or legend of the third degree was now added by Desaguliers when the work was divided into three degrees for the Entered Apprentice, Fellows and Masters. The ancient ceremonies of the Egyptian and Eleusinian mysteries were made use of by him to make the myth or legend of the fate of the master builder of King Solomon's Temple fabricated, for the purpose of concealing by symbolism the death of the Grand Master of the Templars and others who became martyrs for conscience sake, who were victims of that terrible power which for so many centuries has been the curse of mankind.

So says our lamented brother, Albert G. Mackey, of blessed memory: "To few Ma   of the present day, except to those who have made Freemasonry a subject of special study, is the name of Desaguliers very familiar. But it is well they should know that to him, perhaps more than to any other man, are we indebted for the present existence of Freemasonry as a living institution, for when, in the beginning of the eighteenth century, Masonry had fallen into a state of decadence which threatened its extinction, it was Desaguliers who, by his energy and enthusiasm, infused a spirit of zeal into his contemporaries which culminated in the revival of the year 1717, and it was his learning and social position that gave a standing to the institution, which brought to its support noblemen and men of influence so that the insignificant assemblage of the four London Lodges at the 'Apple Tree Tavern' has expanded into an association which now overshadows the entire civilized world. And the moving spirit of all this was JOHN THEOPHILUS DESAGULIERS."

Three years before this revival took place Queen Anne (the second surviving child of James II., who succeeded William III. and her sister Mary II.) died on the 1st Day of August, 1714, the last reigning sovereign of the House of the Stuarts, and was succeeded on the 20th of October following by George I., a Prince of the House of Hanover. This foreign German Prince, who had been born and reared under a different civil state of affairs, upon making an investigation into the condition of his new realm, was totally unable to comprehend the institution of Freemasonry, which socially appeared to be so levelling in its doctrines and principles, and could not understand how a society formed of men with different degrees of rank could meet on the same level—scholars, philosophers and scientists and men from the working guilds of Operative Freemasonry. He was suspicious, fearing that their assemblages might be used for purposes menacing to his reign and in the end conspire for the overthrow of his government, and was disposed to attempt the exercise of his arbitrary and despotic will by closing the Lodges and forbidding their assemblages. However, upon being appealed to and informed that his ideas were erroneous and the cause of his fears groundless, he reconsidered his intentions in that respect, but to satisfy his royal pleasure required that the Masters of Lodges and their successors in office for themselves and the members should take an oath of allegiance especially to him and the House of Hanover, that they would be true and loyal subjects and not engage in plots and conspiracies against him, his family or his Parliament, which oath they were required to take and administer to their successors, which was accordingly done; but it was the first time in its history that Freemasonry, by its officers, were ever sworn to support and tie its fortunes to any line of Kings or household, or to maintain any particular government, and thus commit its destiny to the will and caprice of a sovereign who, if by revolution should be driven from his throne, they themselves, as his sworn adherents, would be forced into exile or suffer imprisonment or such other punishment as might be inflicted by the successful party. The Craft was no longer free, but existed under royal caprice and restraint. This custom, in a a modified form, has been inherited and perpetuated in American Lodges in the installation ceremonies of installing their Masters.

So long as there was a royal bond of unity existing between England and Scotland on account of a member of the House of Stuarts being of the royal family on the throne of England in the persons of James I., Charles I., Charles II., James II., his daughter Mary II., the wife of William III., and Anne, his second daughter, Scotland was measurably quiet; but when Cromwell's iron hand was laid on the throat of Charles I. and a German Prince and foreigner was called to the throne, there was either restive impatience or actual rebellion and revolution in Scotland, the general sympathy of that people going out after one of their own nation who had any sort of a claim to the throne, pretentious or not; and being naturally a warm-hearted people and hot-blooded, their generous sympathy would be manifested for the weaker party in the conflict so long as he wore the plaid, no matter whether he was in the right or not; and especially when a foreigner, and he being only able to speak English in a broken manner with a German accent, hard to be understood.

Freemasonry having now for the first time in its history a regular representative organized government with a national head, its Grand Masters and officers being elected from among its members, it became, as it were, a republic for itself within a kingdom, but sought royal patronage and favor for protection or for policy's sake so as not to give offense to the reigning monarch, who might attempt to close the Lodges or impose restraint upon their organization and limit its operations, which in a manner had already been done. Royalty looked upon Fremasonry to a certain degree with disfavor, and thinking to prevent its increase of numbers a restriction was imposed upon the Lodges and their members, *that no one was to be solicited to join them*—a rule which was never required before, but which has been continued until the present time.

King Solomon said there were "three things too hard for him, yea even a fourth: the way of a ship in the sea, of an eagle in the air, a serpent on a rock, and the way of a man with a maid." So it would have been equally as hard for King George I. to have ascertained how Freemasonry swelled its ranks to so great a number as it did without violating the rule he had, through his ministers, imposed upon the Craft. As has been well said by our late and lamented brother, Albert G. Mackey: "The design of Freemasonry is neither charity nor almsgiving, nor the cultivation of the social sentiment for both are merely incidental to its organization; *but it is the search after truth*, and *that truth* is the *unity of God* and the *immortality of the soul.* The various degrees or grades of initiation represent the various stages through which the human mind passes and the many difficulties which men, individually or collectively, must encounter in their progress from ignorance to the acquisition of this truth."

It was this idea which generally prevailed in the seventeenth century among the Operative Freemasons, who were called upon to construct religious and other edifices for the various sects which had divided the Christian Church, and that called forth a more general spirit of inquiry among them into religious and philosophical truth and the calling to their aid the scientific, philosophic and learned scholars of the age, who were welcomed into the Operative Guild as auxilliaries and were received and made Adoptive or Accepted Freemasons, as had been their custom from time immemorial, and among those admitted was the learned antiquarian, Elias Ashmole, who also has left the impress of his work upon the drama in that portion of the ritual which now relates to the Fellow Craft Degree in particular and before Freemasonry was divided into three degrees. He was made a Freemason October 16th, 1646. Some thirty-six years afterward, on March 10th, 1682, he was summoned to attend a Lodge of Masons the next day at Masons' Hall, London, an account of which he has left in his diary.

Among his collection, to be found in the Ashmolean Museum at Oxford, among other things he says: "There is no doubt to be made that the skill of Masons, which was always transcendent even in the most barbarous times—their wonderful kindness and attachment to each other, how different soever in condition, and their inviolable fidelity in religiously keeping their secret—must expose them in ignorant, troublesome and suspicious times to a vast variety of adventures, *according to the different fate of parties and alterations in government.* By the way, I shall note that the Masons were always loyal, which exposed them to great severities when power wore the trappings of justice, *and those who committed treason punished true men as traitors.* Thus in the third year of the reign of Henry VI. (1432) an Act of Parliament was passed to abolish the society of Masons and to hinder, under grievous penalties, the holding of Chapters, Lodges or other regular assemblies. Yet this act was afterward repealed and, even before that, King Henry VI. and several of the principal Lords of his court became Fellows of the Craft."

In connection with this subject we again revert to the so-called revival of Freemasonry in 1717 and take up the name of three of the Grand Masters of England who followed each other in succession immediately after Desaguliers, viz: The Duke of Wharton, the Earl of Dalkeith and Lord Paisley. These gentlemen, and eminent Masons and Grand Masters, had been attainted and forfeited their titles in the British or, rather, Scotch peerages for their adherence to the House of the Stuarts, as will be seen by reference to De Brett's "Peerage of Great Britain and Ireland." Wharton forfeited his title in 1728. Dalkeith was a descendant of the Duke of Monmouth, illegitimate son of Charles II. Charles Radcliff, who had married Charlotte, Countess of Newburgh, a widow, was the third son of Edward the second, Earl of Derwentwater, and assumed that title upon the death of his nephew, who was executed for rebellion against George II. in 1716, and fleeing to France assisted in the planting of Freemasonry in that country and became the first Grand Master of Masons of France in 1725. His mother was Mary Tudor, the illegitimate daughter of Charles II. He had also been attainted and convicted of treason before his flight. He left France in 1733 (five years before the Grand Lodge of England was organized) and made several visits to England in unsuccessful pursuit of pardon. The blood of the Stuarts, though illegitimate, which flowed in his veins operated as an effective barrier to his hopes and prospects. Baffled with hopeless disappointment, he at last allies his fortunes to those of the Young Pretender in 1745 and sailed from France to join him, but the vessel in which he had embarked was captured by an English man-of-war. He was taken prisoner and beheaded on Tower Hill,

London, December 8th, 1746. [The Fourth Grand Master of California, Charles Morton Radcliff, born at Inverness, Scotland, February 5th, 1818, was his grand-nephew.]

The great monument in London was designed by Sir Christopher Wren, on which he intended to erect the statue of Charles II, instead of the pot of flames as we now see it. But in this he was overruled by men of decency and good sense who did not want to see their country disgraced by the effigy of the most lustful monarch that ever sat on the throne of England, who debauched his people and destroyed virtue.

Perhaps no greater royal libertine ever lived than the infamous Charles II., and incidentally the streams of pure Freemasonry were destined to carry along with them the history of the lives of men who were either legitimately or illegitimately descended from him, or who, by sympathy with the cause of his line of the House of the Scotch Stuarts against that of the successful German and foreign House of Hanover, which for two hundred and thirty years has held the throne of Great Britain, Ireland and its colonial dependencies.

The Scottish Element at the time of the so-called revival of Freemasonry in England prevailed, and the Masonic world is greatly indebted to a man born on August 5th, 1684, at Edinburgh, Scotland—a Doctor of Divinity of the Presbyterian faith, who removed to London and became the pastor of the Scotch Presbyterian Church in Swallow Street, Picadilly—the Rev. James Anderson, who was commissioned by the Grand Lodge of England on the 29th of September, 1721, to collect and compile the history and charges of the Fraternity from the then existing constitutions of the Lodges. "Anderson's Constitutions and Old Charges and Regulations," compiled by him, have been the general standing regulations of the Fraternity for nearly a century and three-quarters since they were collated; and when we consider the troublous times in which the so-called revival of Freemasonry took place in England, the characters of the persons connected with it and the predominance of Scottish noblemen who had their titles forfeited, and Scottish gentry and scholars also connected with it, we naturally and logically conclude that the fountain-head of the Freemasonry then taught and practiced must be looked for in Scotland itself, which had infused its spirit and teachings into the Grand Lodge of England, thus created and governed in the main by Scotchmen, and where the Scottish sentiments and ideas prevailed so largely, as subsequent events proved to be the case as time and circumstances developed them, and the spirit with the ceremonies of the Rosy Cross of the Scottish Templars, modified and adapted to the Master's Degree in Blue Masonry with the invention of the legend of the fate of the Master Builder of Solomon's Temple as a symbol which each could adapt and apply for himself.

The restoration of the widow's son to life by the prophet Elijah; that of the widow's son by the prophet Elisha; that of the widow's son of Zain by Jesus, who also raised Lazarus (the widow's son) from the grave and restored to life, typical of his own resurrection after his crucifixion and death, found delineation and representation by the Scottish Templars in their Order of the Rosy Cross of the widow's son of Mary; to also represent the betrayal and death of De Molay, the last Grand Master of the Templars, by order of Pope Clement V. and Philip the Fair, were to be applied to Hiram Abif, the architect of King Solomon's Temple, as a legend of pure fiction, invented for the purpose of concealing a hidden truth. For there is no history, sacred or profane, which gives any account of the tragical fate of Hiram Abif, either before or after the completion of the Temple, and the last mention that is made of him anywhere in history is in the Scriptural account, as follows:

" So Hiram made an end of doing all the work that he had made King Solomon for the House of the Lord."---*I. Kings, 7:40.*

But the adherents of the House of the Stuarts made the application to Charles I., and while they carried Freema onry to the Continent of Europe, and especially to France, hoping to use it successfully in the cause of the Pretender, in the application of its legend by restoration to power in England, the liberal philosophers and scientists of the Continent who became united to the Fraternity of Freemasonry gave it a broader significance and intention of purpose, and Europe soon was fairly ablaze with the electric lights of intellectual and spiritual liberty, ardently striven for by the lovers of Free Thought and Free Conscience throughout the Continent ; and everywhere the investigation into mental and religious philosophy and the sciences was pursued with an avidity and enthusiasm almost equal to that which had animated the Crusaders to rescue the sepulchre of Christ from the hands of the Saracens.

The histories, myths and legends of all the ancient nations were explored to their depths, and degrees were invented by legions, and rites of initiation were organized by the hundreds, of true and false Freemasonry, many of hem under the direction of the Jesuits, for the purpose of misleading and producing confusion worse than that which caused the stampede at the building of the Tower of Babel. If they could not prevent the true Freemasonry from progressing, yet they by subtilely playing upon the selfish propensities of ambitious men within it, could cause it to be divided, and hoped that of itself it would fall into ruins, and thus eventually be destroyed.

Towards the latter part of the Seventeenth Century, on the 9th of June, 1668 was born at Ayr in Scotland, Andrew Michael Ramsay, the son of a baker who was well-to-do, who gave his son a liberal education in his own town and a the University at Edinburgh. By his great natural ability, diligence and industrious perseverance he rose high in his scholarship to the position of a teacher. He was a Protestant in religion and sought the practice of his profession first in Holland, and was subsequently employed in Paris by James III, the Pretender, as the tutor of his children after he had embraced the Roman Catholic faith. But having while in Holland imbibed the spirit of mysticism, he became the formulator of degrees and the founder of a Masonic rite bearing his name, from which several of the degrees were taken to form other rites and systems of Freemasonry out of the myths, legends, and histories of the ancient nations with that of the Hebrew and Egyptian especially and the Temple of Solomon at Jerusalem as the central idea of concentration as a symbol. In 1728 he visited England with the object of having his system adopted by the Masonic Lodges there, but did not meet with the success he hoped for, and returned to France where he died May 6th 1743, in the seventy-fifth year of his age. But his visit to England was not entirely fruitless as will be seen by the following.

The great majority of the Fraternity in England at that time were come municants of the Established Church. A few were Independents or Congregationalists and Presbyterians, but the greater portion of the minority wer-liberals in their religious sentiments, and governed by a spirit of toleration towards all the various sects. While Ramsay could not succeed in having the English Lodges adopt his system, especially the degree of the Royal Arch of Enoch or Solomon which was also known as the "Grand Scottish Knight of the Sacred Vault of James VI," on account of it being brought from France, and of the national prejudice against the French and hostility to the Stuart Family whom in one sense he represented, yet he planted the seeds of ambition and discord which were to bear fruit in the then near future, which was to rend the Grand Lodge of England asunder, and cause no less than three Grand Lodges to exist at one and the same time and at war with each other.

Personal ambition for office, religious and political as well as personal differences, were the real causes which split the Grand Lodge of England in twain in 1738 while the pretexts for the cause of division were puerile, frivolous and childish. The seceders under Lawrence Dermott called themselves the "Ancient York Masons," without the authority of the Grand Lodge at York, and styled the regular bodies from which they had seceded the "Moderns," and in 1739 set up a new Grand Lodge, dismembered the Third or Master's Degree, leaving that in partial ruins, and carried over the severed portion and deposited it in the ruins of King Solomon's Temple where it was to be found in a newly manufactured degree, made by Dermott called the "Royal Arch of Zerubbabel" to distinguish it from the original Royal Arch of Enoch or Solomon; using the Sacred or Secret Vault second-handed, for the new myth or legend invented by him out of material thus borrowed, to arrange his new system, containing matter and ceremonies of which the remaining members of the original Grand Lodge knew nothing of, nor did their successors in England, until seventy-five years after when, in 1813, these two Grand Lodges united and formed the present Grand Lodge of England which in its declaration of Constitution declared that "Ancient Craft Masonry consisted of the Three Degrees of Entered Apprentice, Fellow Craft and Master Mason only including the Holy Royal Arch."

These two Grand Lodges of England during this long period of three quarters of a century, chartered Lodges throughout the English dependencies and with the Grand Lodges of Scotland and Ireland occupied joint possession of the American Colonies until the war of Independence in 1776 which severed also all Masonic allegiance to the Mother country. The war of the Revolution in America which was successful under the benign influence and direction of Washington, healed the differences between the "Ancients" and "Moderns" in this country, who were still more strongly united together by the additional ties of kindred and patriotism, and the Military Lodges which were formed, added strength and influence to the cause of Freemasonry and to the lovers of liberty from Maine to Georgia. The first of the Military Lodges being "American Union No. 1," which at the close of the Revolutionary War, found permanent lodgment at Marietta, Ohio, the first established west of the Alleghanies, where it still flourishes.

During the middle portion of the Eighteenth Century, while the Continental wars in Europe were in full activity, Freemasonry continued to thrive in spite of the devastation of war and the hostility of nations; and the thunders of the Vatican against it, in the fulmination of the bulls of the Pope, threatening excommunication, confiscation of property, imprisonment and death to all who belonged to the hated and persecuted Order, failed to crush the spirit or destroy the bonds of fraternity which bound it together. During this period English Freemasonry remained comparatively inactive or was engaged in dissensions and bitterness of strife; its power for good rendered inoperative, the true spirit of Freemasonry emasculated, and the two Grand Lodges of England were like tired and exhausted eunuchs, who had become worn out in a boxing or wrestling match in the arena and no longer capable of doing each other harm. But each changed its lectures and formula repeatedly, and English Freemasonry stood still. And it has been well and truly stated by a most distinguished Masonic writer, that at this time "it became envious and suspicious of the higher degrees. It refused to recognize them as Masonic, or to form any connection with them, or with the Royal Arch of Dermott, framed from the Royal Arch of Enoch or Solomon. It never had any object after the struggle of the Stuarts had ended. But Scottish Freemasonry, on the contrary, engaged in its long controversy with Royal and Pontifical Despotism, and became the apostle of Free Thought, Free Speech and Free Conscience."

The Rite of Perfection consisting of twenty-five degrees, was being rapidly extended and propagated throughout France, Italy, Germany and other European States. Frederick the Great of Prussia, though thoroughly a German and devoted to the Fatherland and to the Protestant religion, found himself and his kingdom to be the intended victim and prey of the Pontificate which was intriguing with and stirring up the Roman Catholic nations around him to acts of unfriendliness and hostilities against him and his kingdom. Being an accomplished French scholar, a lover of literature and philosophy and an ardent Freemason, even in the midst of active warfare, he found time to patronize the arts and sciences, to study the occult mysteries of Freemasonry and enjoy the society of the most distinguished philosophers, authors and poets of that age. With the assistance of his Scottish and French brethren and others, for the better protection of Freemasons and the Order in general, he remodeled with with their assistance the Rite of Perfection in its government, and interlacing eight other degrees which were added to it, formulated the Ancient and Accepted Scottish Rite of Freemasonry with himself as its Chief, and established its Constitutions in 1762, which were revised in 1786, and which have been the fundamental law of that Rite to the present date, which is destined to become the most popular, as it is the most universal rite around the globe. It has been plundered and robbed extensively of its degrees, to patch up other rites and systems under other names, and emasculated of their original spirit and objects, and only rendered mechanically dramatic, without the true morals and lessons they were originally intended to teach. "*De mortuis nil nisi bonum*" is a maxim generally adopted to express Masonic Charity for the faults of the dead; but for the survivors Masonic Justice also declares "*De mortuis nil nisi verum.*" Let nothing be said of the dead but what is *true.*

And before entering the next chapter, it will be but right and proper to state that Jeremy L. Cross, in this country, interpolated into the Master's Degree his fiction of the Broken Column and the Weeping Virgin, with old Father Time with his hour glass and scythe, employed in unwinding the ringlets of her hair, from observing that figure in statuary in St. Paul's Churchyard in New York city.

In the same manner he laid hold of the side degrees of Royal and Select Masters of the Ancient and Accepted Scottish Rite of Freemasonry in the jurisdiction of the Southern Supreme Council and propagated them in the territory of the Northern Supreme Council, and established bodies which in time have become representative and legislative, and partially attached to the Webb Chapter and Commandery system.

"The evil that men do lives after them and the good is often interred with their bones."

Thomas Smith Webb, out of the Master Mark Mason's Degree, in part, manufactured the American Mark Master's Degree, invented that of Past Master and Most Excellent Master at Albany, New York, at the same time he revamped Dermott's Royal Arch Degree.

"Most Excellent Master." This degree is peculiarly American, it being practiced in no other country. *It was the invention of Webb*, who organized the capitular system of Masonry as it is taught in this country and established the system of lectures which is the foundation of all subsequent systems taught in America. [Page 511 Mackey's Enc.]

The others he may have had a perfect right to do, but he wronged his English Royal Arch Brethren who did not possess them, requiring them to be "healed," that is, to receive his degrees before they were allowed to visit the American Royal Arch Chapters. This was throwing doubt over the purity of the character of the Mother by the Daughter, who had brought in strange children into the family household only one of which has any claim to beauty or historic accuracy. To meddle with their Royal Arch is questionable. But when he laid hands on the Ancient and Accepted Scottish Rite and took the Fifteenth and Sixteenth Degrees or Knight of the East and Prince of Jerusalem away bodily, degrees that are entirely Hebrew and Persian in their history and drama and 653 years before the crucifixion of Christ, and called the telescoped but purloined degrees the "Red Cross Degree," and took portions of the eighteenth degree, or Rose Croix, and something of the twenty-ninth or Grand Scottish Knight of St. Andrew, and thirtieth or Knight Kadosh, to make his American Knight Templar Degree, he took that which he had no legal right to whatever, and made his confreres and successors the innocent receivers and keepers of stolen property, and wrongfully and with equal impropriety called his Chapter and Commandery system the "York Rite" and made a repetition of a worse character than did Lawrence Dermott when he set up his Grand Lodge of Seceders from the Grand Lodge of England in London and called it the "Grand Lodge of Ancient York Masons" without the least shadow of a claim to the title, for the Grand Lodge of York Masons then still existed at the ancient city of

York. It is evident that he had unlawful access to the rituals of the A. and A. S. Rite deposited in the Archives of the Lodge of Perfection at Albany New York, then dormant, while he resided in that city where he invented his degrees.

But to return to the main subject. Scottish Freemasonry from its foundation to the top of its loftiest spire, is the Temple of Civil and Religious Liberty, teaching and practicing the true principles of Liberty, Equality and Fraternity. "It has the old Knight's Templars for its models, the Rose Croix for its fathers and the Johannites for ancestors." It is the continuer of the school of Alexandria, heir of all the ancient initiations; depository of the secrets of the Apocalypse and the Sohar; the object of its worship is Truth represented by the Light; it tolerates all creeds and professes but one and the same philosophy. The allegorical object of Freemasonry is the rebuilding of the Temple of Solomon; its real object is the reconstruction of social unity, by the alliance of Reason and Faith in accordance with knowledge and virtue, with initiation and tests by means of degrees, and we may add to preserve the natural liberties and rights of Man, corporeal, intellectual and spiritual against all usurpations of royalty and Sacerdotal power.

Said that implacable enemy of Freemasonry and the mouthpiece of Pope Pius VI, the Abbe Barruel, in 1797. Charging the Freemasons with revolutionary principles in politics and with infidelity to the Roman Catholic religion seeking to trace the origin of the Institution to those ancient heretics the Manicheans and through them to the old Knights Templars, against whom he revives the old accusations of Philip the Fair and Pope Clement the Fifth, he said: "Your whole school and all of your Lodges are derived from the Templars. After the extinction of their Order, a certain number of guilty knights having escaped proscription, united for the preservation of their horrid mysteries. To their impious code they added the vow of vengeance against the kings and priests who destroyed their Order and against all religion (papal) which anathematized their dogmas. They made adepts, who should transmit from generation to generation, the same mysteries of iniquity, the same oaths and the same hatred of the God of the Christians (*the Pope*) and of kings and of *priests* (*papists*). These mysteries have descended to you, and you continue to perpetuate their impiety, their vows and their oaths. Such is your origin. The lapse of time and the change of manners, have varied a part of your symbols and your frightful systems; but the essence of them remains; the vows, the oaths, the hatred, and the conspiracies are the same."

So far as the origin of our Freemasonry and Lodges are concerned in being derived from the Ancient Templars, and hatred of temporal and spiritual tyranny being taught as toward such monsters as Philip the Fair and Pope Clement the Fifth with the tortures of the Inquisition, the fanatical and bigoted Abbe Barruel was correct; but as to the falsehood and slanders against the Fraternity, we do not know of a more fitting reply than that made by the author of the Grand Constitutions of the Ancient and Accepted Scottish Rite of Freemasonry, Frederick the Great, to be found in the following account which will close this Chapter.

In the year 1778, during our American Revolution for Independence,

Frederick the Great of Prussia, and the friend of Washington, whom he admired as a patriot and Freemason, and to whom he sent the present of a sword and for whom Fredericksburg, Virginia, was named, found trouble in his own dominions which he promptly suppressed.

The Superior of a Dominican Convent at Aix-la-Chapelle, Father Greineman and a Capuchin Monk, Father Schiff, were trying to excite the lower classes against the Lodge of Masons at that place, which had been reconstituted by the Mother Lodge at Wetzlar. When Frederick heard of this, he wrote the following letter, dated February 7th, 1778, to the instigators.

"Most Reverend Fathers: Various reports confirmed through the papers, have brought to my knowledge with how much zeal you are endeavoring to sharpen the sword of fanaticism against quiet, virtuous people called Freemasons. As a former dignitary in this honorable body, I am compelled as much as it is in my power, to repel this dishonoring slander, and remove the dark veil that causes the temple we have erected to all virtues, to appear to your vision as a gathering point for all vices. Why, my most reverend Fathers, will you bring back upon us those centuries of ignorance and barbarism, that have so long been the degradation of human reason? Those times of fanaticism, upon which the eye of understanding cannot look back but with a shudder? Those times in which hypocrisy, seated on the throne of despotism with superstition on one side and humility on the other, tried to put the world in chains and commanded a regardless burning of all those who were able to read.

"You are not only applying the nickname of Masters of Witchcraft to the Freemasons, but you accuse them to be thieves, profligates, forerunners of Anti-Christ, and admonish a whole nation to annihilate such a cursed generation."

"Thieves, my most reverend Fathers, do not act as we do, and make it their duty to assist the poor and the orphans. On the contrary, thieves are those who rob them sometimes of their inheritance, and fatten on their prey, in the lap of idleness and hypocrisy. *Thieves cheat, Freemasons enlighten Humanity.*"

"A Freemason returning from his Lodge, where he has only listened to instructions benfitted to his fellow beings, will be a better husband in his home. Forerunners of Anti-Christ would in all probability, direct their efforts toward an extinction of Divine Law. But it is impossible for Freemasons to sin against it, without demolishing their own structure. And can those be a cursed generation, who try to find their glory, in the indefatigable efforts to spread those virtues, which constitute them honest men?

FREDERIC."

John L. Pavkovich,

CHAPTER III.

BRIEF HISTORY OF THE RITE OF PERFECTION AND OF THE
ANCIENT AND ACCEPTED SCOTTISH
RITE OF FREEMASONRY.

Before entering direct upon the History of the Ancient and Accepted
Scottish Rite in particular, it is well perhaps to give a brief sketch of the Rite
of Perfection from which it is mainly derived.

By whom or when all the degrees of the Rite of Perfection were brought
into existence, history is totally silent upon. They seem however to have been
the best of all the degrees of Freemasonry that survived the great mortality of
"La Grippe" which befell the legions which came into existence during the
first half of the last century; adopting the language of St. John, the Apostle, in
speaking of the Acts of Christ "which if they shall be written every one, I
suppose that even the world itself could not contain the books that should be
written," while King Solomon, though dead for nearly 3000 years, has been
worked corporeally and made a phonograph of since his decease to talk myriads
of times more than he did when he was alive, and tradition in his case has
been made perennial and exhaustless, a thousand fold greater than the stories
and jokes accredited to the lamented Abraham Lincoln.

Some of the degrees of the Rite of Perfection were brought out by Ramsay, and others by Benedictine Monks who became disgusted with their Order
and abandoned it; one of whom, Antoine Joseph Pernetty, a native of France,
who like thousands of others was warmly received by Frederick the Great,
who made him his librarian.

It may be well said, that the Monk of Eisleben of Germany was the
"Great Pioneer and Torch Bearer of the Reformation to bring out the Great
Light which had been hidden and concealed in the monasteries of Europe for
Centuries. When Martin Luther released the Bible from its chains in his
monastery and from the fetters of a dead language not understood by the common people, and it was given to the world literally on the wings of the prin-
ter's press, he prepared the way to unlock the treasuries where the wisdom and
knowledge of the centuries had been imprisoned for ages, which came forth
liberated and disenthralled. The myths and legends of history and tradition,
with the arts and sciences and philosophy, that burst forth from their prison
cells, and, like birds just out from their cages, by natural instinct had to look
around for a place to perch and for safety; and it was found under the protect-
ing wings of the Black Eagle of Germany and in the person of Frederick the
Great.

But to defeat the purposes of Freemasonry, the Jesuits had managed to inveigle themselves into it, that they might eventually obtain the control, divert it from its objects and in the end destroy it.

In 1754, the Chevalier de Bonneville (not Nicholas) established a Chapter of the High Degrees at Paris in the College of Jesuits of Clermont. He was not the founder but the propagator of them. The College of Clermont was the asylum of the adherents of the House of the Stuarts; and hence the Rite of Perfection from that source became to some extent, tinctured with Stuart Masonry. It consisted of twenty-five degrees. In 1758, the degrees of the "Rite of Perfection" were carried by the Marquis de Bernez to Berlin and they were adopted by the Grand Lodge of the Three Globes; and the same year when the Jesuits who thought they had suppressed it, the Rite again made its appearance in Paris under the authority of the "Council of Emperors of the East and West." Between the years 1760 and 1765, the Jesuits, finding they had not destroyed it as they expected to, again insinuated themselves as they always had done and will ever continue to do, where it is possible, and sowed the seeds of dissension and a new organization called the "Council of the Knights of the East," was formed; and a rivalry and contention existed between these two bodies and the Grand Orient of France, until finally in 1781 both were absorbed in that Grand Body which held in France the Rite of Perfection within its bosom.

It however continued to flourish in Germany under Frederick the Great, who gave it its Grand Constitutions in 1762. After a trial of twenty-four years, finding that it was necessary to re-organize or reconstruct the Rite and to lift it up still higher in the scale of philosophy and its teachings, and to prevent its control from again falling into the hands of the Jesuits, he interlaced and added eight other degrees to it, and named the new and reformed system "THE ANCIENT AND ACCEPTED SCOTTISH RITE OF FREEMASONRY." and established the Grand Constitutions which were ratified and signed at Berlin on the first of May 1786.

Up to that time from 1762 under the former Constitutions, he was Grand Commander of the Order of Princes of the Royal Secret and the Supreme Chief of the Scottish Rite or of Perfection.

By these Constitutions of 1786 he resigned his authority and his Masonic prerogatives were deposited with a Council in and for each nation, to be composed of Sovereign Grand Inspectors Generals of the Thirty-third and last Degree of legitimate Freemasonry limited in number to that of the years of Christ on the earth.

On the 25th of October, 1762, the first Grand Constitutions (framed in that year) were finally ratified at Bordeaux, and proclaimed for the government of all the Lodges of Sublime and Perfect Masons, Councils, Colleges and Consistories, of Sublime Princes of the Royal Secret over the two Hemispheres. This was done with the consent and approval of the Grand Consistory at Berlin. In 1761 the Scotch Rite or of Perfection, (afterwards known as the Ancient and Accepted Scottish Rite) was brought to America by a Frenchman, Brother Stephen Morin, in accordance with the powers with which he had been invested by the Grand Consistory of Sublime Princes of the Royal Secret, convened at Paris on the 27th of August, 1761, under the Presidency of Chaillon de Joinville, Substitute General of the Order.

When Morin arrived at San Domingo, agreeable to his patent and according to his instructions, he appointed Brother Moses M. Hayes as a Deputy Inspector General for North America, with the power of appointing others wh rever necessary. Brother Morin also appointed Brother Franckin as a Deputy Inspector General for Jamaica and the British Islands and Brother Colonel Provost for the Windward Islands and the British Army. The Constitutions of 1762 being transmitted to Brother Morin soon after their adoption and ratification by the Grand Consistory of France, who furnished duly authenticated copies of the same to all the deputy Inspectors Generals appointed by him and his Deputies, and are still in force, as far as they are not modified and repealed by those of 1786.

Brother Franckin instituted a Lodge of Perfection of the Fourteenth Degree at Albany, New York, on December 20th, 1767 (nine years before the Declaration of Independence) and conferred the Degree of Sublime Prince of the Royal Secret (then the 25th Degree but now the 32nd), upon a number of Brethren, but this body after its creation remained comparatively dormant for many years, and its original warrant and books of record and patents of Brethren, were fifty-five years after its establishment discovered and brought to light in 1822 by our late Brother Giles Fonda Yates. This was the first body of the Rite of Perfection planted on the Continent of North America. From its rituals and material it no doubt aided Thomas Smith Webb to formulate his system of degrees in the Royal Arch Chapter, to appropriate the 15th and 16th degrees entire, to make his Red Cross Degree as he did, and, from the Rose Croix and other material with his own invention to make the American Knight Templar Degree, for he resided at Albany in the years of the interim and prepared his system there.

Other material from the Rite was also appropriated by Jeremy L. Cross and then the property was left concealed where Brother Yates found it. Brother Yates by due authority revived it, and placed it under the superintendency of a Grand Council of Princes of Jerusalem as required by the Old Constitution of 1762 and such Grand Council was subsequently opened in due form in that city.

Brother Hayes in 1781, appointed Brother Da Costa Deputy Inspector General for South Carolina, Solomon Bush for Pennsylvania, and Brother Behrend M. Spitzer for Georgia, which appointments were confirmed by a Council of Inspector General on the 15th of June, 1781, two years before the close of the Revolutionary War. After the death of Brother Da Costa, Brother Joseph Myers was appointed by Brother Hayes to succeed him.

Before Da Costa died, he in accordance with the Constitutions of 1762 established a Sublime Grand Lodge of Perfection in Charleston, in the year 1783, where for the first time in the United States of America, were the Degrees actually worked from the 4th to the 14th inclusive; for in this Country the three symbolic degrees of the Blue Lodge being under the control and government of the Grand Lodges by which they were established, their authority duly recognized by all legitimate Scottish Rite Brethren in this Country who have remained true and loyal in their allegiance to the sovereign powers of

Ancient Craft Masonry, which in turn appoints representatives to and receives from the regular legitimate Councils of the Ancient and Accepted Scottish Rite of Freemasonry in various countries of the world, and are in amity with them.

On the 20th of February, 1788, a Council of Princes of Jerusalem was duly constituted at Charleston and the officers installed by Brother Joseph Meyers, Behrend M. Spitzer and A. Frost.

The researches into the early history of the planting of the Scottish Rite or that of Perfection in this country, prove that notwithstanding the appointment of Inspectors Generals in the several States the Rite was worked in Charleston only, and to the zeal of our Charleston Brethren (the most of whom were of Huguenot descent) to their constant application to the Scottish Rite, are we indebted for the foundation of the first Bodies of the Rite in America, and the parent of all legitimate Bodies of the Scottish Rite now in existence.

In 1796, a Council of Knights Kadosh, (of the 30th degree) was organized in Philadelphia by Brethren who had fled thither from the West Indies. This Council soon after became extinct through the return of its founders; and in 1797, a Chapter of Rose Croix (of the 18th degree) was founded in New York City.

On the 17th of August, 1786, Frederick the Great died and he was succeeded by his son Frederick William III, who was not a Mason. In France the Rite of Perfection was condensed into seven degrees called the "*Rit Moderne*," or the "Modern French Rite with the seventh or highest degree, the Rose Croix." The condition of France and of French Freemasonry was in constant ebullition and trouble; and in the terrible upheaval and Revolution in 1798 of that people, everything civil, judicial, political and Masonic were in a state of unutterable confusion, conflict and chaos.

The Constitutions of 1786 however, had been received by the Brethren at Charleston, South Carolina, as well as the rituals of the eight degrees which had been added by the authority of Frederick the Great to the Rite of Perfection, now constituted into the "Ancient and Accepted Scottish Rite of Freemasonry." But the Rite of Perfection in a mutilated and sickly condition continued to exist in the West Indies where remnants of the Bodies were scattered.

Although the Revolutionary War in America had been successful and the United States had been established on a sure foundation with a Constitutional Government, yet it was comparatively in its infancy. In some portions, Freemasonry under different and civil Grand Lodges, the inheritors of their English Grand Lodge progenitors was still unsettled and a hostile feeling manifested for many years. There were two opposing Grand Lodges in South Carolina, one the "Ancients" and the others the "Moderns." In this state of affairs the Brethren of the Rite of Perfection in Charleston in that State, found themselves between two fires, and without a Supreme head to their own Rite existing anywhere; and as related by Sir Walter Scott in Quentin Durward, one of the Waverly novels, in the reply made by Quentin Durward to Charles, Duke of Burgundy when he said, "And that, finally, when I did avail myself of that imputed character, it was as if I had snatched up a shield to protect myself in a moment of emergency and used it, as I surely should have done for the defense of myself and others, without enquiring whether I had a right to the heraldic emblazonments which it displayed."

So it was with the Brethren at Charleston, they were in possession of the Grand Constitutions of 1786 as well as those of 1762, together with the rituals of the new Rite, formed as the "Ancient and Accepted Scottish Rite," and the new Rite and Grand Constitutions of 1786, became their shield of protection and defense, by their appropriation and adoption, which action no power on earth then existed to dispute their right to them; and the first Parent Supreme Council now existing, which was formed agreeably to the Constitutions of 1786 was that founded at Charleston, South Carolina, on the 31st of May, 1801, by Brothers John Mitchell and Frederick Dalcho, the former a Colonel in the American Army and the latter a Protestant Clergyman and a most distinguished writer.

[It is well to note at this point that up to this time, the Dermott Royal Arch Degree had not been severed from the Blue Lodges of the "Ancients" which alone worked it and none of Webb's degrees had then been made by him at Albany, New York, namely the Mark Master, Past Master and the Most Excellent Master, Red Cross, Knights Templar and other degrees, nor had the Mark been carried to England at that time.]

The Supreme Council having been established at Charleston as above stated, it was the first Supreme Council of the world and became the mother and grandmother of all other legitimate Councils that were brought into existence, after it was first established and which with itself are the only legal authority of the Ancient and Accepted Scottish Rite in America or elsewhere.

In 1802 it conferred the 33d degree on Brothers Count de Grasse Tilley, Hacquet, and de la Hogue; and these Brethren by its authority of Letters Patent dated February 21st, 1802, established the Supreme Councils of France and those of the French and English West India Colonies. The Supreme Council of France was duly installed by Ill. de Grasse Tilly, on the 22d of December 1804, at Paris, in the hall known as the Gallery of Pompeii, situated in the Rue Neuve des Petits Champs. This Supreme Council was the first and only one established in France, and it was afterwards divided into two branches, one called the Supreme Council of France and the other the Supreme Council of the Grand Orient of France. These two bodies are still in existence; but the former only is in relations of comity with the Mother Supreme Council, (which created it,) and all the other regular Supreme Councils of the world.

Ill. Brother de Grasse Tilly also established the Supreme Councils of Italy, Naples, Spain and the Netherlands.

Article V. of the Grand Constitutions of 1786, provides that there shall be only one Supreme Council of the 33d degree in each Nation or Kingdom; two in the United States of America, as distant as possible one from the other, one in the British Islands of America and one also in the French Colonies.

As already stated, the First Supreme Council which was created under those Constitutions was that of Charleston, South Carolina. It began its labors on the 31st of May, 1801, and its jurisdiction extended over the whole United States of America, until the 5th of August, 1813, when it established the "Supreme Council of the Ancient and Accepted Scottish Rite of Freemasonry for the Northern Jurisdiction of the United States," through its special proxy and representative, Emmanuel de la Motta. This Supreme Council whose M. P. S. Grand Commander was Brother D. D. Tompkins, Vice-President of the United States of America, replaced the Grand Consistory of Sublime Princes of the Royal Secret 32d Degree which had been established by the same authority on the 6th of August, 1806. Subsequently in after years the seat of the Northern Supreme Council was removed to Boston. Its jurisdiction embraces all the Northern or Northeast quarter of the United States east of the Mississippi River (excepting the small eastern fraction of Minnesota,) and embraces the States of Maine, New Hampshire, Vermont, Massachusetts, Rhode Island, Connecticut, New York, New Jersey, Pennsylvania, Michigan, Ohio, Indiana, Illinois and Wisconsin. All the rest of the States and Territories were reserved by the Supreme Council for the Southern Jurisdiction of the United States, which Masonically remained undisturbed and unaffected by the acts of secession of the Southern States, which formed the Southern Confederacy during the late Civil War.

The Supreme Council for the Northern Jurisdiction of the United States of America, created the Supreme Council of England and Wales in March. 1846, and this Body in its turn created the Supreme Councils of Scotland and of the Canadian Dominion, the Southern Supreme Council creating the Supreme Council for Ireland.

The labors of the two regular Supreme Councils of the United States of America and their subordinates have never been interrupted and from the first day of their creation, up to this time, both have enjoyed the rights and privileges of Supreme Councils, as the constituent and administrative heads of the Ancient and Accepted Rite, each in its respective jurisdiction and whenever an attempt has been made to invalidate their authority and prerogatives, it has been met with a denunciation of the individuals or bodies encroaching upon their rights. Since, therefore, the 5th of August, 1813, the provisions of Article V of the Constitutions of 1786 have been complied with, and there are in the United States of America consequently but two Supreme Councils, They have ever preserved and enforced their authority, and they have never failed to discountenance all attempts against an authority which rightfully *ab initio et de jure et de facto* belongs to them.

It was impossible for a third Supreme Council to be established in the United States of America, without violating the Constitution of 1786, without which, as already stated, neither the 33d Degree nor Supreme Council can exist. It was an unwise measure to have established a second Supreme Council in the United States, even though it was permissible by the Constitutions, as subsequent events have proved. It was a strange historic coincidence, that the very year that saw Blue Masonry in England of the two Grand Lodges there consolidated into one, that Scottish Freemasonry in the United States, should have even amicably divided into two separate organizations, each Supreme Council altering and amending its own Constitutions and Statutes and changing and making alterations of its rituals, destroying the harmony and uniformity of the work.

But at that time there were no railroads or steamboats, and the distances being so great, difficult modes of conveyance accompanied with great expense and loss of time in travelling to and from the places of meeting and the country again in war with Great Britain was at that time considered a good excuse for the establishing of a second Supreme Council; and it will be a happy day for the Rite, when both Supreme Councils shall again be consolidated into one "National Supreme Council of the Ancient and Accepted Scottish Rite of Freemasonry" for the United States of America, and which all true lovers and well wishers of the Rite desire to see accomplished as soon as practicable.

The evil fruits of the division were soon apparent, and both Supreme Councils were soon put on their defense against the invasion of imposters and frauds, which did not effect Scottish Rite Masonry alone, but Grand Lodges of Blue Masonry, Grand Royal Arch Chapters and even Grand Commanderies of Knights Templars, spurious bodies of which were also established as well as of the Scottish Rite by these impostors.

We do not intend to waste ink, paper and valuable time to trail up all of the acts of these frauds and their dupes and give a history of the spurious Councils and other bodies created by them; yet it would be unwise not to acknowledge that they have had an existence and that some still exist to be used as tools by the Jesuits for the purpose of destroying Freemasonry in general, or crippling its efforts to benefit our country and mankind.

At this point it may not be out of place to quote from a letter of the late Ill. Bro. Dr. Henry Beaumont Leeson, the Sovereign Grand Commander of the Supreme Council of England and Wales and their Dependencies, written at London in 1860 to the Grand Commander of the Southern Supreme Council of the United States. He says:

"Our own Council is now in a flourishing condition, nearly all of the elite of Masonry in England being ranged under our banners; and although we are distinct from Grand Lodge, who acknowledge only the first three degrees and the Royal Arch, and Grand Conclave, governing the Knights Templars. These two last degrees are in this country, perfectly different and distinct from any of the Ancient and Accepted Degrees, *and of very modern origin, neither having existed previous to the middle of the last century.* ☞ *The Knight Templar Degree was concocted in France* AND I POSSESS THE ACTUAL MINUTES AND OTHER RECORDS OF THE FRENCH CONVENT. The Royal Arch (Dermott's) was concocted by Ramsay, and modernized by a Chaplain (G. Brown) of the late Duke of Sussex." (Grand Master.)

It was this spurious French Knight Templar Degree, and different from the Webb Templar Degree, that was not only carried to England and established there, but was also brought to the United States by the French imposter, Joseph Cerneau, who made spurious Templars in New Orleans as well as he did in New York, where he and his co-adjutors also established spurious Bodies of Templars and of the Rite of Perfection with twenty-five degrees, and by the hocus-pocus of jugglery shifted and changed the names of his Bodies from time to time, as suited his pleasure and by mere *dicta per se* alone, declared himself and his co-adjutors Sovereign Grand Inspectors Generals of the 33d degree. A clandestine Lodge of Fellow Craft Masons might with equal propriety resolve themselves into a Grand Lodge of Master Masons, without ever having even clandestinely been raised to the Sublime Degree of Master Mason at all.

Unfortunately, afterwards, the Northern Supreme Council for a few years was divided into two factions which the impostors took advantage of and one of these factions compromised with and affiliated some of the dupes of these frauds, and took them in, and when the schism or breach was afterwards healed, the Northern Supreme Council for a time was infected with an unhealthy absorption by an unwise compromise which was made with the best intentions for the good of Freemasonry.

Some of these frauds had been the means of splitting even the Grand Lodge of New York in twain, and the original chief of them, this French adventurer and impostor had previously represented the spurious Knight Templars of New Orleans and the spurious Council of the Rite of Perfection of Louisiana in the Grand Encampment of Knights Templar of New York, as we quote from the records. "On the 4th day of May, 1816, a meeting of the Grand Encampment of Knights Templar of New York, was called to act upon an application by a collected body of Sir Knights Templar, Royal Arch Masons, *and members of the Sov. Grand Council of Sublime Princes of the Royal Secret for the State of Louisiana, sitting at New Orleans* praying that a constitutional charter be granted them, etc. They had previous to this application elected and installed their officers. The charter, by resolution, was granted them, and it was also

Resolved:—That the *Ill. Bro. Joseph Cerneau*, having been designated by the Louisiana Encampment to be their representive and proxy near this Grand Encampment, be and is hereby acknowledged and accredited as such.

Thus in this manner this spurious French Templar Degree that was carried from France to England, got into the United States, through the back door as it were, at New Orleans, and allied with a spurious Rite and Body and is amalgamated with the American Webb Templar Degree at New York and all regular Freemasonry within that State becomes inoculated with the poison, which still rankles in the veins of some who are still leprous and beyond the reach of hope for their recovery, *for they have shown themselves to the priest too often.*

To suppress the evil it has required the united efforts of all the regular bodies of Freemasonry, Grand Lodges, Grand Chapters and Grand Commanderies of Knights Templars as well as both of the regular and legitimate Supreme Councils of the United States, to quarantine it, and then destroy it; but it is a leprous cancer and poisons all who come in contact with it or who try to apply mild remedial applications, when only constant heroic treatment can eradicate it. *There is a Jesuit at the root of it.*

Yet in spite of all of these evils which have beset the Ancient and Accepted Scottish Rite of Freemasonry, it has made great advance and is prospering; and during the past five years in the Northern Jurisdiction alone, it has increased nearly fifty per cent. in numbers and the returns of the Supreme Council for the Northern Jurisdiction of the United States for September, 1889, shows the following:

Parenthetically we may remark that in spite of persecutions and Brethren being imprisoned for no other reason than that they were Freemasons, yet under the Supreme Council of Colon, Cuba, there are no less than *three* Consistories of the 32°, *seven* Councils of Kinghts Kadosh 30°, *thirty-four Chapters of Knights Rose Croix 18°*, *thirty-four Councils of Princes of Jerusalem 16°* and *thirty-four Lodges of Perfection 14°* in the Island of Cuba "the Gem of the Antilles," alone! And this too where but a few years ago our Brethren were butchered and murdered at their altars.

We will now revert to the Supreme Council for the Southern Jurisdiction of the United States with which we have been officially and otherwise connected as subordidate to and a Deputy Inspector General at times for a period of nearly a quarter of a century. In the Southern Masonic Jurisdiction, the Rite suffered severely from the misfortunes incident to the late civil war. Its treasury was exhausted in Masonic charity, its records and rituals lost and burned in the conflagration of Charleston, (the birthplace and home of our late Brother Mackey, its Secretary General,) and other cities, and at the close of the war but few Bodies had any existence, and the Brethren who had not died, were scattered and left impoverished, so that it seemed almost impossible to resuscitate the Rite in that portion of its jurisdiction.

There is something inexpressibly sad and touching as we read the records of the last two meetings of the Supreme Council for the Southern Jurisdiction of the United States held previous to the late civil war and those immediately after it. That of March 28th to 31st of 1860 held at the City of Washington. Of the nine active members who assembled then, only two survive, the present Grand Commander Albert Pike, and the Secretary General Fred Webber. The last act of that session was to pay a pilgrimage to Mt. Vernon, escorted by Washington Commandery of Knights Templar, and hold a Lodge of Sorrow in honor of the memory of George Washington, the Father of his Country, a little more than a year before the flames and explosions of the civil war were to burst forth over the land. The session of April 1st in 1861 was held at New Orleans when twelve of the officers and active members were present, of whom only three are now living, Brothers Pike, Webber, and Batchelder.

At the session of February, 1862, at Charleston, only four were present, no business transacted, and all are dead. War was then raging in all its fury, and Freemasonry apparently dead, and "silence prevailed in all the valleys," while tears flowed in that dark hour from the eyes of men unused to weep.

The Southern Supreme Council did not meet again until after the close of the war, and in the Masonic Hall in Charleston, South Carolina, on November 17th, 1865. Only six members were present and all but one of them, the present Grand Commander Albert Pike, have crossed over the river. Excepting in New Orleans there were no Bodies of the Rite working anywhere. The ravages of war had swept everything away, and all was sadness, sorrow and ruin, and for the moment a feeling of hopeless despair pervaded the breasts of this half dozen veterans of the Rite.

The Northern Supreme Council was then divided in twain and impostors and frauds were like jackals gorging themselves upon the battlefield upon the bodies of the slain. *"Ardet ut vivat."* "She burns that she may live," was once a motto of the old Knights Templars, and the Phœnix was again to rise from the ashes of the funeral pyre. For, with the indomitable energy and zeal of it Illustrious Sovereign Grand Commander, Albert Pike, 33°, who had during the last two years and a half of the war, been engaged in rewriting and restoring its rituals, whose matchless scholarship in ancient lore and profound knowledge of the Ancient Mysteries and philosophy, aided by that other most illustrious Mason, the Moses and Lawgiver of the Fraternity of Freemasons around the Globe, Albert Gallatin Mackey, 33°, the late Dean and Secretary General of the Southern Supreme Council, assembling like Zerubbabel and Haggai with a few others at the ruins of their Temple at Jerusalem, commenced the reconstruction of the Rite at Charleston, South Carolina, upon the old foundations which remained undisturbed. Though the Temple and City were destroyed, yet their jurisdiction of the Holy Empire remained intact. Without money and means they devoted themselves to the work. That portion of the jurisdiction which before had been comparatively unoccupied, and happily escaped the ravages of war, and the black cloud of sorrow and desolation which covered the southern and eastern portions of their jurisdiction, still moistened with blood and wet with the dew of tears of the sorrowing and afflicted, had a silver and even a golden lining when lifted by the fresh breezes from the Pacific shores, borne across the Sierras' and the Rocky Mountains' crest, to the woe-stricken hills and valleys of the South.

As has already been stated, nearly all the Bodies of the Rite in the Southern Jurisdiction were either dead or dormant, and the work of resuscitation and reconstruction was a most herculean task to attempt or accomplish; and in the midst of it there arose opposition and bitter controversy from ignorance and prejudice which continued for many years, until it was happily allayed, the error acknowledged by those other Brethren who wantonly assailed the Rite, but who afterwards became its most vigorous and ardent defenders.

On the Pacific Coast, the late Ill. E. H. Shaw, 33°, Active Inspector General for California, aided by Ill. Thomas H. Caswell, 33°, (now also Active Inspector General for California and Grand Chancellor of the Southern Supreme Council), in 1866 to 1870, established twenty Bodies of the Rite in California including the Grand Consistory of which the writer became the Grand Registrar and since that time Inspector General Caswell has established one other Body of the Rite in California, besides doing a very large amount of work in advancing the interests of the Rite on the Pacific Coast.

In Oregon, in the same period, Ill. John C. Ainsworth, 33°, then Active Inspector General of that State, aided by the late E. H. Shaw, 33°, established six Bodies of the Rite in that State.

The latter also established four Bodies of the Rite at Virginia City in the State of Nevada, in 1867, and in 1871, one at Salt Lake City, in Utah Territory.

The writer as the Deputy of the late E. H. Shaw, 33°, constituted one Body at Hamilton, White Pine County, Nevada, in 1871, and as the Deputy of Ill. Thomas H. Caswell, 33°, one body at Eureka, California, in 1871.

As the Deputy of the Southern Supreme Council in 1872 he established fifteen Bodies of the Rite on Puget Sound in the then Territory but now State of Washington. In 1874 and 1875 he assisted in the organization of the two Bodies of the Rite, one above the other at Carson City, Nevada, and was installed Master of both.

In October, 1883, he assisted in organizing three Bodies of the Rite in Oakland, California, of which he became a Charter member and the Commander of the Council of Kadosh of which Bodies he is still a member and an officer in each, being at present the W. Master of the Chapter of Rose Croix.

(The Grand Commander having conferred the degrees upon a class of twelve members previously, who formed about one third of the charter members when constituted).

Ill. Charles F. Brown, 33°, having for many years rendered most efficient service to the Rite by untiring zeal, devotion and perseverance, and worked his way up from the onerous position of Master of Ceremonies of the Lodge of Perfection to that of Venerable Master of the same, and through the Oriental chairs of the various other Bodies, to the office of Venerable Grand Master of the Grand Consistory of California, which he honored by his efficiency and zeal, was at last rewarded by being elected and crowned as an Active Member for the State of California, in the Southern Supreme Council.

As his Deputy, the writer, in the year 1885, constituted four Bodies of the Rite in California and as the Deputy and Grand Lecturer of the Grand Consistory (of which he is still an officer) he visited and instructed the various Bodies of the Rite in the interior and on the borders of the State of California.

During the last twenty-two years the writer has been a charter member and officer of no less than *nine* Bodies of the Rite, a member and officer of four others and as a Deputy has constituted *twenty-one* other Bodies of the Rite in California, Nevada and the State of Washington, making *thirty-five* Bodies in all consisting of one Grand Consistory 32°, one Subordinate Consistory 32°, *six* Councils of Kadosh 30°, *nine* Chapters of Rose Croix 18°, *six* Councils of Princes of Jerusalem 16°, and *twelve* Lodges of Perfection 14°, with which as a member and an officer he has been identified, while he has participated in the initiation of many hundreds of Master Masons into the Rite, upon a large proportion of which he has himself officially conferred all the degrees from the 4th to the 32nd inclusive. As a recognition of the long sixteen years of service previously rendered to the Rite, the Southern Supreme Council by unanimous vote at its session in October, 1884, elected him a Knight Commander of the

Court of Honor and to receive the Thirty-third Degree as an honorarium, and an Honorary Member of that Supreme Council, which was duly conferred upon him.

At the time of the Triennial Conclave of the National Grand Encampment of Knights Templars of the United States, held in San Francisco in August, 1883, the Grand Consistory of California welcomed and entertained at their parlors in the Palace Hotel, no less than 480 Scottish Rite Bre.hren of the 32nd degree, visitors to the Pacific Coast borne upon its register, while the utmost spirit of courtesy and fraternity prevailed; and delegations from California Commandery, No. 1, and Golden Gate Commandery, No. 16, of Knight Templar visited the Scotttsh Rite headquarters, which were returned by the Grand Consistory in full uniform, accompanied by the 2d Regiment Band.

There is no ground or cause for envy, jealousy or conflict existing between the two Rites, and only the ignorant, narrow-minded and bigoted, who are incapable of receiving more light, whose capacity is already filled, and they can hold no more, are like lamps filled with wicking, with but a small space for oil, give but little light, soon burn out, and end in darkness and smoke.

The Supreme Council of the Southern Jurisdiction has now removed its headquarters to Washington City, District of Columbia. It owns its own asylum, which belongs to all the members of the Rite alike, in its jurisdiction, and where its business may be transacted, and official and fraternal intercourse held with every Mason, who will always find a cordial welcome under its roof Its constituency is constantly and steadily increasing, with nearly two hundred regularly organized bodies of the Rite over its widely extended territory. and nearly approaching in number of members that of its more prosperous Sister Council of the Northern Jurisdiction, which did not suffer by calamities of war.

To the late Ill. E. H. Shaw, 33°, Thomas H. Caswell, 33°, Charles F. Brown, 33°, Active Inspectors General for California, Theodore H. Goodman; 33°, Stephen Wing, 32°, George J. Hobe, 33°, and others of California; Ill. John C. Ainsworth, 33°, John McCracken, 33°, Rockey P. Earhart, 33°, Active Inspectors General, and Irving W. Pratt, 33°, and Christtopher Taylor, 33°, Honorable Inspectors General and others for the State of Oregon, and Ill. James S. Lawson, 33°, Active Inspector General for the State of Washington (now of California), James G. Hayden, 33°, and others of that State, is the Rite mainly indebted for its success on the Pacific Coast, whose influence and power is daily being augumented, and its mission being steadily performed. It confers no degrees but what are strictly and legitimately its own, and its doors are open to every worthy intelligent Master Mason, who is seeking for knowledge and light, and who is willing to use the sword when necessary in the defense of the trowel in the building of the temple of civil and religious freedom, where the principles of Liberty, Equality, and Fraternity are inculated, and where the loftiest truths of science and philosophy are taught, and the religion of humanity without creed, and politics without party, are most studiously cultivated. A ladder like that in Jacob's dream, where the Christian, the Jew, the Mohammedan, the Brahmin, and even a Buddhist brother may climb to its summit and view the Infinite, and hold communion with the All Father if he so desires, without encroaching upon the rights and privileges of his brother Mason.

It is this spirit of toleration which the Rite inculcates, and like the bee gathers honey from every flower for the common hive, yet carries a weapon to defend itself when attacked in its course by the oppressor, the thief, and the robber in every land.

The illustrious names of Parvin, Tucker, Jordan, Teller, Carr, Browne, Batchelor and others, shine brightly over the plains east of the Rocky Mountains, from British America to Mexico, from the Ohio River to the Gulf and from the majestic Mississippi to the storm-beaten shores of the Atlantic; while the index finger of Liberty from the dome of the Capitol of the Nation beckons the members of our Supreme Council to assemble, and beneath the shadow of the loftiest monument ever erected to the memory of man, the "Father of His Country" and the "Father of American Freemasonry, our own beloved Washington, who received the gift of his sword from Frederick the Great, who gave us our Grand Constitutions, of the Ancient and Accepted Scottish Rite, and in whose honor the city of Fredericksburg, Virginia, was named, and in our own jurisdiction.

Of the legitimate Supreme Councils duly recognized by each other around the globe entitled to fraternal recognition, are the following:

Southern Jurisdiction, U. S. A.	Constituted	May 31,	1801
*France (Supreme Council)	"	Sept. 22,	1804
Northern Jurisdiction, U. S. A	"	Aug. 5,	1813
Belgium	"	March 11,	1817
Ireland	"	June 11,	1825
Brazil	"	April 6,	1826
Peru	"	Nov. 2,	1830
New Grenada	"	———	1833
England, Wales and Dependencies	"	March	1846
Scotland	"	———	1846
Uruguay	"	———	1856
Argentine Republic	"	Sept. 13,	1858
Turin, of Italy	"	———	1848
Colon (Cuba)	"	———	1855
Venezuela	"	———	1864
Mexico	"	Apr. 28,	1868
Portugal	"	———	1842
Chili	"	May 24,	1862
Central America	"	May 27,	1870
Hungary	"	Nov. 25,	1871
Greece	"	June 24,	1872
Switzerland	"	March 30,	1873
Canada	"	October,	1874
Rome, of Italy	"	Jan. 14,	1877
Egypt	"	———	1878
Spain	"	———	1879
Tunis	"	May 11,	1880
Canada	"	———	———

*The Grand Orient of France is not in fraternal communion with any Masonic body of the United States.

The following Supreme Councils have been formed, but have not received formal recognition and the courtesy of an exchange of representation: Naples of Italy, Dominican Republic, Turkey, Palermo of Italy, Florence of Italy, and Luxemburg.

To several of these Supreme Councils the Grand Lodges of the maritime States of the Atlantic and Pacific Coasts appoint representatives to and receive representatives from, they being also Grand Lodges and governing the blue degrees. But in the United States, England, Scotland and Ireland, the government of the symbolic Lodges and the control of the blue degrees are relinquished to the Grand Lodges of their several jurisdictions.

But to receive the degrees of the Ancient and Accepted Scottish Rite in the United States, *it is only necessary to be a Master Mason in good standing*, and the degrees of the Scottish Rite commence from that of Master Mason, and are regularly conferred in legally constituted bodies of the Rite, at or in the vicinity of the applicant's residence, if there be any; or they are conferred by communication by Active Inspectors General of the 33d degree of the Rite, or by their duly appointed Deputies, who are authorized to communicate them and create members at large, as *nuclei* for others to be afterward constituted into bodies when there are a sufficient number, the fees received being paid into the Charity fund, after deducting the necessary expenses of the Supreme Council.

While it may be considered a large number of degrees, yet the lessons and catechism to be learned are very short, not averaging over five questions and answers to a degree, in order to be perfect. Yet the patent, or diploma, will at all times admit the lawful possessor to any body of the Rite which he is entitled to visit by virtue of the rank of the degree to which he has attained.

The following is the scale of degrees of the Ancient and Accepted Scottish Rite, and are designated as follows. The Ineffable Degrees pertain to King Solomon's Temple only.

The Ineffable Degrees conferred in a Lodge of Perfection are:

4°, Secret Master,
5°, Perfect Master,
6°, Intimate Secretary,
7°. Provost and Judge,
8°, Intendant of the Building,
9°, Knight Elect of the Nine,
10°, Illustrious Elect of the Fifteen,
11°, Sublime Knight Elect of the Twelve,
12°, Grand Master Architect,
13°, Royal Arch of Solomon,
14°, Grand Elect Perfect and Sublime Mason,

Which have sole reference to all the events in detail, in regular order in connection with the completion and dedication of King Solomon's Temple, and which may be classified as follows: The 4th and 5th have relation to the proper tribute due to the memory of the third Grand Master of the Temple. The 6th, 7th and 8th, to supplying the place made vacant by the death of the Architect of the Temple, in keeping the record of the plans agreed upon by the two kings, the adjustments of the accounts and demands of the workmen, the settlement of disputes, and the resumption of work upon the Temple.

The 9th and 10th to the faithful administration of justice, which never tires or sleeps. The 11th, the rewardingof the faithful and true for bringing offenders to justice, and the regulation of the equitable collection of the revenues of the realm. The 12th, the science of architecture, the use of all the instruments and their morals, and the science of astronomy, with geometry and the lofty lessons to be learned in the study of the starry heavens above us. The 13th, the fortunate discovery of that which have been lost, but unknown to the discoverers; and the 14th, the preparation of the mind, heart and body by consecration to the service of true Freemasonry, and to receive, with the fullest and most ample explanations, the great treasure and reward on the competion of the Temple, which is delivered by the two kings to the patient, discreet, and faithful workman, which will enable him in all his journeys through life to be welcomed and received as a true brother, earn his wages and the bread for himself and his family, and to contribute to the relief of his fellows.

NOTE.—From the Sixth Degree and a portion of the history of the Fourteenth Degree, the Degree of Select Master was made. And from the Thirteenth and Fifteenth Degrees, with a change of history, applied to the second Temple under Zerubbabel, left unfinished, Lawrence Dermott made his Royal Arch when he split the Grand Lodge of England in twain, in 1739, and added to by Dunckerly, when he dismembered the Master Masons Degree and cutting off the True Word and attaching it to the Royal Arch, and remodeled by Webb, is the Royal Arch Degree of the American Rite as practiced in the United States as heretofore stated.

SECOND TEMPLE DEGREES.

The following are the Second Temple Series:

15°, Knight of the East, of the Sword or of the Eagle.

16°, Prince of Jerusalem.

These two degrees are founded upon the history of the two reigns of the Persian monarchs, Cyrus and Darius, the destruction of the Temple of Solomon by Nebuzuradan, the captivity of the Jews, who were carried away into Babylon, the decrees of these two kings permitting the rebuilding of the Temple by Zerubbabel and the restoration of the holy vessels, and the release of the Jews from captivity, with the hindrances and opposition from the Samaritans, all serving to symbolize the destruction of the Order of the Temple which was ruined, scattered and proscribed, and of a country which has once lost its liberties, and the difficulty of regaining them, teaching to Freemasons, as brethren, the lessons of patience and perseverance under affliction and trials, and never to despair in their efforts to regain that which, through treachery, persecution, oppression and robbery, whether of liberty or possessions, they, like the old Knights Templars, may have lost.

NOTE.—These two degrees were taken bodily by Webb, from the Ancient and Accepted Scottish Rite, telescoped or consolidated by him and called the "Red Cross Degree" and placed by him in the American Commanderies of Knights Templar, without leave or license. They are entirely Jewish and Persian in history and drama and the events occurred 563 years before the Crucifixion of Christ, as already stated.

KNIGHT OF THE EAST. The Fifteenth Degree of the Ancient and Accepted Scottish Rite. It is also substantially the Tenth Degree or *Knight of the Red Cross of the American Rite.* [Page 415, Mackey's Enc.]

KNIGHT OF THE RED CROSS. "Webb, or whoever else introduced it into the American system, *undoubtedly took it from the Sixteenth Degree or Prince of Jerusalem of the Ancient and Accepted Rite.*

It has within a few years, been carried into England under the title of the "Red Cross of Babylon." In New Brunswick it has been connected with Cryptic Masonry. It is there as much out of place as it is in a Commandery of Knights Templars." [Page 418, Mackey's Enc.]

BABYLONISH PASS. A degree given in Scotland by the authority of the Grand Royal Arch Chapter. It is also called the Red Cross of Babylon and is almost identical with the Knight of the Red Cross conferred in Commanderies of Knights Templar as a preparatory degree. [Page 99, Mackey's Enc.]

EMBASSY. The embassy of Zerubbabel and four other Jewish chiefs to the court of Darius to obtain the protection of that monarch from the encroachments of the Samaritans, who interrupted the labors in the reconstruction of the Temple, constitutes the legend of the Sixteenth Degree of the Ancient and Accepted Scottish Rite, and also of the Red Cross degree of the American Rite, *which is surely borrowed from the former.* [Page 250, Mackey's Enc.]

THE SPIRITUAL TEMPLE DEGREES.

17°, Knight of the East and West.

18°, Knight Rose Croix (or of the Rosy Cross.)

The 15° and 16° embraced in the Council of Jerusalem are now, with the 17° and 18°, conferred in the Southern Jurisdiction, in the Chapters of Rose Croix.

The 17° of Knight of the East and West portrays the history and life of St. John the Baptist and his sad fate like that of the Master Builder of Solomon's Temple, who fell a victim and a Martyr to the principles of virtue, integrity and truth; and also the history and teachings of St. John the Evangelist, the Beloved Disciple who, in his gospel, declared that "in the beginning was the Word, and the Word was with God and the Word was GOD," and whose rapturous vision of the New Jerusalem on the Isle of Patmos, in which he was told to "weep not, behold the Lion of the tribe of Judah, the Root of David hath prevailed," made him the Knight of the West to proclaim the truth in revelation as John the Baptist had been the Knight and Herald of the East, at the head of the Order of the Essenes, to declare the approach of "One that cometh after him, and who is preferred before him."

The 18°, or Rose Croix, portrays the history of him who came to elevate his race and to be the Reformer and Redeemer of Men. One whom all liberal minded men, regardless of creed, will readily admit was unjustly and inhumanly put to death, as a victim to satisfy the clamors of a fanatical mob, at the instigation of a hierarchy that was false to its race, and content to willingly serve under the foreign yoke of a conqueror, to pay tribute to its power, that priestly authority might control the destiny of its own people whom it

was willing should be kept in subjection that they might, with a rod of iron,
rule over the hearts and consciences of men. A hierarchy that finds to-day
its counterpart at the Vatican in Rome. In the 18° no violence is done to any
man's religious faith, while the Christian may draw its lessons more closely to
heart than others; yet the grand principles of Toleration, Humanity and Fraternity are taught, in which all good men may recognize Christ as a Most Wise
Master Builder, and one endeared to us as "our elder Brother," who has taught
us to say "Our Father which art in Heaven," and to "Do unto others as we
would have them do unto us."

NOTE.—From the Rose Croix Degree, Webb made his Knight Templar Degree
in part.

THE HISTORIC, PHILOSOPHIC AND CHIVALRIC DEGREES.

19°, Grand Pontiff.
20°, Grand Master of all Symbolic Lodges.
21°, Noachite or Prussian Knight.
22°, Prince of Libanus, or Knight of the Royal Axe.
23°, Chief of the Tabernacle.
24°, Prince of the Tabernacle.
25°, Knight of the Brazen Serpent.
26°, Prince of Mercy.
27°, Knight Commander of the Temple.
28°, Knight of the Sun, or Prince Adept.
29°, Grand Scottish Knight of St. Andrew
30°, Knight Kadosh, or of the Temple.

The 19th degree relates to the Apocalyptic Vision of St. John the
Evangelist, and the hoped-for millenium, when there shall be a perfect union
of mankind under the perfect sway of Toleration and Charity.

The 20th degree teaches Veneration for the Deity, Knowledge, Science
and Philosophy, inculcates Charity, Generosity, Heroism, Honor, Patriotism,
Justice, Toleration and Truth.

The 21st degree portrays the history of the Knights Crusaders, who
returned to Europe from the wars in the Holy Land, to find themselves and
their kindred stripped of their properties by the rapacity and cunning frauds
of the Monks, and the recovery of their lands, and the punishment meted out
to those cowled thieves and robbers who plundered the estates of the living
and dead, and the absent defenders of the Faith in Palestine, and turned old
men, women and children out upon the highways to starve and perish by the
roadside.

The 22d degree relates to the work upon Mt. Lebanon, and the preparation of the timbers and woodwork for the Temple; the dignity of labor, and
that in Freemasonry rank and nobility go for naught, and that he who will
not work among his fellows in the Craft, shall not eat.

The 23d and 24th degrees relate to the history of the formulation of the
ceremonies of the Jewish religion, in the setting up of the Tabernacle in the
Wilderness, and the doctrines and laws given by Moses, who was well versed
in all the knowledge of the Egyptians.

The 25th degree portrays the sufferings of the Children of Israel, who were bitten by fiery serpents in the Wilderness, and the raising up of the brazen serpent by Moses, that those who looked upon it might live, in which the profoundest doctrines are taught of life and death, and to lead men away from their evil passions and to look for help and relief from above.

The 26th degree particularly treats of mercy, charity and loving kindness, of toleration, and that men are not to be persecuted and tortured on account of different creeds or faiths, all of which is exemplified by recounting the sufferings and woes inflicted for religious differences of opinion in the ages that are past.

The 27th degree relates to the Crusades under Henry VI, of Germany, son of Frederic Barbarosa, aided by all the knighthood and chivalry of Europe, joined by Philip Augustus of France, and Richard Cœur de Lion of England, which went to the Holy Land in 1191, and became the Teutonic branch of the Order of the Temple, and known as the Knights of St. Mary, where they established a Hospital on Mount Sion, for the reception of pilgrims. The lessons taught to fight for the glory of Masonry, to uphold its banners and vindicate its principles; to love, revere and preserve liberty and justice; and to favor, sustain and defend the oppressed, without neglecting the sacred duties of hospitality.

The 28th degree treats of science and philosophy, and inculcates the full exercise of intelligent reason and faith in the reading of the Book of Nature, with a well grounded trust in the wisdom and mercy of the Creator.

The 29th degree portrays the history and valor of the Scottish Branch of Knights Templar, or Grand Scottish Knight of St. Andrew; the inculcations of a spirit of humility, patience and self-denial, with charity, clemency and generosity based upon virtue, truth and honor, and to resist all oppression, whether it proceed from temporal or spiritual authority, and to recover that which was lost through persecutions, robbery and death, inflicted by those powers which destroyed the Order of the Temple and plundered it of its lawful possessions, giving a portion as a reward to their enemies, the Knights of St. John of Jerusalem, now known as the Knights of Malta.

The 30th degree relates to the history of the Order of the Temple, their woes, sufferings, banishment, destruction and death, and bears the same relation to the Knight Kadosh, that the 3d degree does to Master Masons, or the 18th degree to Knights Rose Croix, with this difference, that it is vastly more profound in its depth of meaning, and more determined in its aims and objects. It is the areopagus and citadel of Freemasonry. It neither attacks or defends any man's creed or religious faith, but it maintains the rights of conscience, freedom of speech, and free government. The horrors of the past, committed by crowned and mitred tyrants, crushing out the souls of men and trampling liberty in the dust, are neither forgotten or forgiven, so long as oppression and wrong from temporal and spiritual despots are permitted to exist and curse the sons of men. Liberty, Equality and Fraternity are its cardinal tenets, with the warning ever in view, that "Eternal vigilance, education and enlightenment are the life and guarantees of liberty."

NOTE. The 30th Degree or Knight Kadosh, [Kadosh Kadoshim, the Sanctum Sanctorum or Holy of Holies of the Temple] is the real Knights Templars' Degree, which in no wise resembles the American-Webb-Templar, or the spurious French Jesuit or Cerneau Templar Degrees, in ceremony, ritual, teachings or dress. As no one under the inflexible rule of the REAL ORDER OF THE TEMPLE or "Poor Fellow Soldiers of King Solomon's Temple or of Jesus Christ," could be admitted and created a Knight Templar *unless he was of noble blood*, the remnant of Knights Templars after the Battle of Bannockburn in Scotland, June 24th, 1314, and after having been created by Bruce, Knights of the Rosy Cross and Knights Grand Crosses of St. Andrew of Scotland, they created the Order of Knights Kadosh, to be composed of themselves and those they saw proper to admit to their fellowship and confidence, after having tested their patience, fidelity and courage. And as they could no longer be known as Knights Templars, they chose the name of Kadosh, the better to conceal their identity for personal safety; and they also assumed the name of Knights of the Black and White Eagle, the black and white having reference to the colors of the pavement of King Solomon's Temple, and of their lost Beauseaut, while the Eagle was the symbol of Liberty, as in the same manner the guild of Operative Freemasonry, *adopted* or *accepted* as Brothers and Fellows, those admitted of the speculative and philosophic Freemasonry.

It is greatly to be regretted that their true name of Knights Templars should have been dropped; but being sensitive and proud of their blood and achievements and history, they preferred to let the true name or title go down in honor and to be obscured by the adoption of a new one, Knight Kadosh, not dreaming that other persons of another age and another land across the Atlantic, not then discovered, should presume to take their names, titles and consolidate them with those of their enemies, the Knights of Malta, unwarrantedly use emasculated portions of their work, and ignorantly but innocently flaunt their insignia and banners before the world, without lineage of blood or lawful inheritance of their ancient rights, honors and privileges, and without carrying out the objects and purposes of the Old and True Knights Templars, as faithfully delineated by their true successors, the Knights Kadosh, in the degrees of the Ancient and Accepted Scottish Rite of Freemasony by its regular and legally constituted authorities. Happily, however, the error is being rapidly corrected by the swelling of the ranks of the Scottish Rite, by those who have also received the Webb and Cross System of degrees, more appropriately denominated by our late and lamented Brother, Albert G. Mackey, 33°, as the "American Rite," who rose to the highest distinction in both Rites. As Napoleon once said, "If you prick a Russian, you bleed a Tartar," so it may be said with nearly equal truth, if one should happen to prick an intelligent Knight Templar of the American Rite, who has attained any distinction at all, he would find that he was drawing the blood of a Rose Croix Knight, or of a Knight Kadosh of the Ancient and Accepted Scottish Rite of Freemasonry, the Parent of all true Masonic Knighthood, Philosophy and Chivalry.

In connection with this subject, the writer disclaims any hostility to a Rite long established, with which he himself is connected and when it is too late to remedy the original wrong or correct the error; but he believes in the motto, "*Magna est Veritas et prevalebit*," and that in writing the history of Freemasonry impartially and unbiased, that "the *truth*, THE WHOLE TRUTH, AND NOTHING BUT THE TRUTH," should be stated, clear from the fountain head; "nothing extenuated and naught set down in malice."

Compensation is being made by the manly, chivalric and Masonic support being given by the Grand Lodges, Grand Royal Arch Chapters and Grand Commanderies of American Knights Templars, in recognizing the legality and regularity of both the Southern and Northern Supreme Councils of the Ancient and Accepted Scottish Rite of Freemasonry, which so far as they are concerned at the present day, is ample atonement for the infringement and wrongs perpetrated nearly a century ago by Webb, Cross and their coadjutors, for which their ignorant and innocent successors are in no wise to be held responsible.

CONSISTORIAL AND JUDICIAL DEGREES.

31°, Grand Inspector Inquisitor Commander.

32°, Master of the Kadosh, or Prince of the Royal Secret.

The 31st degree is the highest judicial degree and Supreme Court, so to speak, of the Rite, in which all appeals are heard, and the trials of all cases above the rank of the 30th degree. The lessons taught are of the highest order of justice, in which the examples of Moses and the principal law givers of the ancient nations are represented and cited, and it is the most august tribunal held in Freemasonry, to teach the loftiest principles of Truth, Equity and Justice.

The 32d degree teaches the ancient truths and philosophy of our Aryan ancestors as they have come down to us drained through the Alexandrian school of science, and the Zoroastrian doctrines; the fundamental principles of the Mosaic and Christian dispensations, the resurrection of the body and the immortality of the soul, with all the symbolism of our ancient brethren left as monuments to guide us in our investigation and search after truth.

The plan of battle to resist the encroachments and attacks of our enemies, with the entire body of Freemasonry in all of its divisions united as a whole, by means of its symbolic geometric formation and combinations of its mysterious numbers.

NOTE.—In the jurisdiction of the Northern Supreme Council, the Council or Preceptory of the Knights Kadosh is within the bosom of the Consistory, while in that of the Southern they are separate.

The rituals of the degrees differ materially in their drama and while that of the Northern Jurisdiction applies more direct to the scenes and history of the Crusades, requiring the skill of the athlete and adroit to delineate the drama represented, those of the Southern Jurisdiction are more intellectual, historic and philosophical, which do not require the experts of a gymnasium to represent its physical development to the sacrifice of the intellectual. The Rite, in the latter jurisdiction has a higher culture for its initiates and seeks rather to instruct, than to astonish and amuse. But the refined scholar as well as the most robust and athletic gymnast, can find sufficient food in both jurisdictions for thought, as well as to enlarge the porosity of his cuticle in sudorific physical exercise; but he will find a wider sphere for his development in the Camp of the Saracens, in paying his physical devotions to the Deity of the Mystic Shrine, which is in no wise Masonic in any sense, but an acrobatic descent from the sublime to the ridiculous, and instead of the war-horse of the Crusader, the bareback of the bucking wild ass of the desert forms the inverted crescent to bestride instead of the steed of Richard of the Lion Heart.

In the Northern Jurisdiction, Councils of Deliberation are held in each State of all the bodies from the 14th to the 32d degree inclusive, presided over by a Deputy for the State, in which all local legislation is presented and acted upon, to be afterwards approved, annulled or amended by the Supreme Council.

In some of the States of the Southern Jurisdiction and Japan, there are Grand Consistories which govern the Bodies the of Rite in their respective states, limited only by the Grand Constitutions and the Statutes of the Supreme Council. In other states the highest bodies are particular Consistories, with no power of government over any other Bodies of the Rite below themselves.

THE GOVERNING DEGREE.

33°, Grand Master of the Kadosh or Sovereign Grand Inspector General.

The 33d degree is conferred in the Supreme Council of the Rite, which is the governing body over all, which prescribes its laws and statutes for the various divisions into which the organized bodies are divided. The active members are limited to thirty-three, including the officers, who for their respective States are relatively the Grand Masters of the Rite. Honorary Inspectors General, are those who are elevated to the degree, but have no other powers than those specifically delegated to them, or they are appointed as Special Deputies to propagate the Rite by communicating the degrees and the establishing of bodies. In all other respects they are like delegates in Congress, with the right to a voice, but not to a vote.

In the Southern Supreme Council the Statutes limit the number of Active Members of the 33d Degree to 33 and no more. In the Northern Supreme Council to just double the number or 66.

In the Southern Supreme Council there is what may be called the Vestibule to the Thirty-third Degree, called the "Court of Honor," which is composed of two grades or ranks and each Active and Emeritius Member of the Supreme Council is *ex-officio*, a member of both grades. The first grade is that of Knight Commander, which is conferred for general meritorious services supposed to have been rendered to the Rite, and is conferred upon Brethren of the 32d Degree, upon the recommendation of the Grand Consistories or by the Active Inspectors Generals of their respective States. The second or highest grade is that of Knight Grand Cross which, with the jewel, is conferred upon Brethren of the 32d degree for extraordinary service and merit in the Rite. Both of the grades of honor are reserved and cannot be conferred upon any person who may ask for them. When conferred, it is an act of gratuity and appreciation for service rendered.

It is necessary to have the rank of Knight Commander of the Court of Honor, in order to be eligible to receive the Thirty-third Degree.

In the Southern Supreme Council there are 29 Active Members, with four vacancies to fill. There are nine Emeriti or Retired Active Members, and 205 Honorary Members, making in all 243 Members of the 33d Degree. The number of Knights Grand Crosses is 75, and Knights Commanders of the Court of Honor of 32d degree is 205.

There are under the jurisdiction of the Southern Supreme Council four Grand Consistories of the 32d degree, one each in Louisiana, Kentucky, California and the Empire of Japan. There are also 13 Particular or Subordinate Consistories throughout the Jurisdiction, including one at Honolulu in the Hawaiian Islands. There are 28 Councils of Kadosh of the 30th degree. Of Chapters of Rose Croix, of the 18th degree 47, and of Lodges of Perfection of the 14th degree 81.

As the territory of the Supreme Council of the Southern Jurisdiction covers so vast an extent, and some of the Bodies of the Rite, are too remote for Brethren Master Masons who may desire to receive the degrees without travelling great distances and at enormous expense, the Active or Deputy Inspector Generals are authorized by the Statutes, to confer the degrees by communication, and place them on the Subordinate Roll of the Supreme Council as Members-at-large, with the direction at the first favorable opportunity, when afterwards residing in the vicinity of regular subordinate Bodies of the Rite, they must make application for affiliation therewith. It is fair to presume that ten per cent. of the membership of the Rite in the Southern Jurisdiction are members-at-large, and as the Rite is a Propaganda within the Body of Freemasonry, this is permissible as well as obligatory, upon all Active and Deputy Inspectors Generals and Bodies of the Rite, but no person not already a Master Mason and in good standing can be admitted to "THE ROYAL AND MILITARY ORDER OF THE HOUSE OF THE TEMPLE," which is the true title of the "ANCIENT AND ACCEPTED SCOTTISH RITE OF FREEMASONRY.

The above concludes all the information that is permitted to be given concerning the Rite which, for the beauty of its ritual, the splendor of its drama, profundity of its philosophy and ethics, the activity put in force in the promulgation of its principles, which have now spread over the whole earth, its perfectness of system, the high character of its membership, which embraces liberal kings on their thrones, the nobility and best scholars of Europe and America, the elite of the Fraternity around the globe, with whom the most modest but intelligent Master Mason may find companionship, receive and impart instruction and feel at home, to whom its doors are open, and whose way up its staircase leading to science and philosophy, to its halls where Gallileo, Copernicus and Kepler would have delighted to tread, and, like Humboldt, find a place for rest and repose, without the shadow of a familiar of the Inquisition to darken the entrances or summon to trial in the torture chambers, where the body is made to suffer for the breathing of the thoughts that are generated by the aspirations of the soul.

In conclusion, it is but proper to reiterate that the Scottish Rite which has doubled its numbers in the past five years and continually increasing, confers no degrees but its own, and has no conflict with any legitimate bodies of any other Rite of Freemasonry to which so many of its members belong. It commends itself to the thoughtful Masonic student as worthy of his study and research in which he will find the truth, and the reward for the time expended in his investigations, that of the Philosopher's Stone.

NOTE:—By way of explanation it may be stated, perhaps, as one of the reasons for the slight difference of the manner of the working of the degrees of the Rituals of the Rite between the Southern and Northern Jurisdictions, and changes which had to be necessarily made, the late Ill. Brother Azariah T. C. Pierson, 33°, Active Inspector General for the State of Minnesota, in the Southern Jurisdiction, shortly before his decease, in November, 1889, informed the writer "that the late Masonic firm of Macoy and Sickles, of New York City, both of whom are 33°, and belong to the Northern Supreme Council, printed the rituals for the Supreme Council of the Southern Jurisdiction as well, but who unfortunately failed in business, and that the stereotype plates which belonged to either or both regular Supreme Councils, were surreptitiously seized upon and taken by persons connected with the Cerneau fraud, who claimed that they had bought them with the rest of the property of Macoy and Sickles, which was sold for the benefit of their creditors; and that it was with these stereotype plates of the rituals thus surreptitiously obtained that the fraudulent Cerneau Supreme Council was thus enabled to improve its own meagre skeleton, and give its subordinate bodies a semblance of the true work conferred under the authority of the regular Supreme Councils, which for self-protection against impostors and clandestine Scottish Rite Masons, had to call in all the rituals then out, and to issue new ones in lieu thereof." If such be the case, and believing it to be true, it will account for the ease and facility of making dupes by the impostors by presenting to them a counterfeit coin containing so large a percentage of the true metal in its manufacture, and the great difficulty of convincing Brethren not belonging to the lawful and legitimate jurisdictions, of the Cerneau impostures as being frauds and their victims who could not believe themselves to be swindled or that they had been clandestinely made.

Fortunately the evil is fast being overcome, and the true and legal authorities of the Rite sustaining themselves with the moral support of all other regular Bodies of Freemasonry throughout the world.

The foregoing completes the labors of the writer in the true history of Freemasonry in general, and of the Ancient and Accepted Scottish Rite in particular, briefly but carefully presented.

Fraternally Yours,

EDWIN A. SHERMAN, 33°,

Hon. Insp. Gen. and the late Special Deputy and Grand Lecturer of the Grand Consistory of California. Hon. Mem. of the Southern Supreme Council, Secretary of the Masonic Veteran Association of the Pacific Coast, etc., etc., etc.

OAKLAND, CAL., June 1st, 1890.

TABLEAUX OF OFFICERS AND ACTIVE MEMBERS

OF THE

Supreme Council of the Southern Jurisdiction
of the United States.

*Register of Subordinate Bodies, Supreme Council of the 33°,
A. & A. S. Rite of Freemasonry, Southern
Jurisdiction, U. S., 1890.*

*Tableau of the Supreme Council of Sovereign Grand Inspectors-
General, 33°, for the Northern Masonic Jurisdiction
of the United States.*

*Grand Bodies, Ancient and Accepted Scottish Rite, Recognized by
the Supreme Councils, 33°, of the Southern and Northern Jurisdictions of the U. S.*

*Roll of Officers and Members of the Masonic Veteran Association
of the Pacific Coast, Etc., Etc., Etc.*

TABLEAUX OF OFFICERS AND ACTIVE MEMBERS

OF THE

Supreme Council for the Southern Jurisdiction of the United States.

Officers.

Grand Commander............ALBERT PIKE............Washington City, D. C.

Lieut. Grand Commander..JAMES CUNNINGHAM BATCHELOR
New Orleans, La.

Grand Prior....................PHILIP CROSBY TUCKER.......Galveston, Texas

Grand Chancellor............THOMAS HUBBARD CASWELL
San Francisco, Cal.

Grand Minister of State...ERASMUS THEODORE CARR
Leavenworth, Kan.

Secretary General............FREDERICK WEBBER...Washington City, D. C.

Treasurer General............JOHN MILLS BROWNE..   "   "   " "

Grand Almoner...............ROBERT CARREL JORDAN...Omaha, Nebraska

Grand Auditor.................SAMUEL MANNING TODD....New Orleans, La.

Second Grand Auditor......WILLIAM OSCAR ROOME, (33° Hon.)
Washington City, D. C.

Grand Constable..............ODELL SQUIRE LONG.........Wheeling, W. Va.

Grand Chamberlain.........MARTIN COLLINS....................St. Louis, Mo.

First Grand Equerry.......JOHN QUINCY ADAMS FELLOWS
New Orleans, La.

Second Grand Equerry.....JAMES RUDOLPH HAYDEN.......Seattle, Wash.

Grand Standard Bearer...BUREN ROBINSON SHERMAN...Waterloo, Iowa

Grand Sword Bearer........GILMORE MEREDITH.............Baltimore, Md.

Grand Herald.................HENRY MOORE TELLER......Central City, Col.

Grand Tiler....................WILLIAM REYNOLDS SINGLETON, (33° Hon.)
Washington City, D. C.

Active Members.

THEODORE SUTTON PARVIN...Iowa City, Iowa

JAMES SMYTHE LAWSON...San Francisco, Cal.

DE WITT CLINTON DAWKINS..............................Jacksonville, Florida

MICHEL ELOI GIRARD...Lafayette, La.

CHARLES FREDERICK BROWN..,..............................San Francisco, Cal.
ROCKY PRESTON EARHART...Salem, Oregon
EUGENE GRISSOM... Raleigh, N. C.
JAMES DANIEL RICHARDSON..................................Murfreesboro, Tenn.
SAMUEL EMERY ADAMS...Minneapolis, Minn.
RUFUS EBERLE FLEMING...Fargo, N. Dakota
ADOLPHUS LEIGH FITZGERALD.................................. Eureka, Nevada
JOHN FREDERICK MAYER...Richmond, Va.
NATHANIEL LEVIN...Charleston, S. C.
RICHARD JOSEPH NUNN.......... ....Savannah, Georgia
GEORGE FLEMING MOORE.....................................Montgomery, Alabama

Emeriti or Retired Active Members.

CLAUDE SAMORY....................... ....New Orleans, La.
GEORGE B. WATERHOUSE, now in New York ....North Carolina
JOHN C. AINSWORTH, now in Oakland, Cal. ....Oregon
JOHN MCCRAKEN...Portland, Oregon
ABRAHAM E. FRANKLAND, now in New York ....Tennessee
WILLIAM ROBERTS BOWEN, now in Pennsylvania ....Nebraska
JOHN LONSDALE ROPER...Norfolk, Virginia
ROBERT S. INNES...................................:............................Minnesota
ACHILLES REGULUS MOREL, now of Oakland. Cal. (9)............Louisiana

Honorary Members.
ALABAMA.

STEPHEN HENRY BEASELEY...Montgomery
FAY MCCULLOCK BILLING (2).................................   "

ARIZONA.

MERRILL PINGREE FREEMAN (1)...Tucson

CALIFORNIA.

ALEXANDER GURDON ABELL...........................San Francisco
ISAAC SUTVENE TITUS... "   "
ELISHA INGRAHAM BAILEY, Surgeon U. S. Army............ "   "
GEORGE JOHN HOBE... "   "
THEODORE HENRY GOODMAN............. .... "   "
AYLETT RAINES COTTON................................... "   "
PETER THOMAS BARCLAY..........   .... "   "
DAVID BERNARD JACKSON.. "   "
COLUMBUS WATERHOUSE....................... .... "   "
CHARLES THOMAS HANCOCK............... .... "   "
WILLIAM ABRAHAM DAVIS.......... .. .. "   "
JOHN MASON BUFFINGTON................................ .... Oakland
EDWIN ALLEN SHERMAN............................ ....   "
DAVID MCCLURE....................................... ....   "
NATHAN WESTON SPAULDING..... ....   "
WILLIAM FRANK PIERCE............. ....   "
CHARLES EDWIN GILLETT................. ....   "
JAMES BESTOR MERRITT...   "

CHARLES MEDLEY DOUGHERTY...Alameda Co.
CHARLES JACOB R. BUTTLAR...Eureka
SILAS MONTGOMERY BUCK...	"
CHARLES E. STONE..Marysville
WILLIAM FRANKLIN KNOX..... ....Sacramento
WILLIAM MONROE PETRIE..	"
JAMES ROBERT DUPUY	(26)..Los Angeles

COLORADO.
LAWRENCE NICHOLS GREENLEAF.....................................Denver
EDWARD CARROL PARMELEE..Georgetown
RICHARD W. POMEROY	(3)..	"

DISTRICT OF COLUMBIA.
CLEMENT WELLS BENNETT..Washington
EDWARD FITZKI...	"
JOHN FRAZIER HEAD...	"
REV. WILLIAM AUGUSTUS HARRIS...................................	"
CHRISTOPHER INGLE...	"
ABNER TOWNSLEY LONGLEY..	"
EDWIN BALRIDGE MAC GROTTY.....................................	"
LUTHER HAMILTON PIKE..	"
WILLIAM OSCAR ROOME..	"
WILLIAM SMITH ROOSE..	"
JOHN ERNST. CHRISTOPHER SCHMID................................	"
THOMAS SOMERVILLE..	"
JOSEPH CLARENCE TAYLOR.......................................	"
JOHN WILSON..	"
WILLIAM W. UPTON...	"
JAMES LANSBURY...	"
THOMAS GEORGE LOOCKERMAN	(17)................................	"

GEORGIA.
JAMES EMMET BLACKSHEAR..Macon
ANDREW MARTIN WOLIHIN..	"
THOMAS WHITTY CHANDLER.......................................Atlanta
CALVIN FAY	(4)..	"

GERMANY.
J. IGNATIUS HIRSCHBUHL	(1)....................................Baden Baden

HAWAIIAN ISLANDS.
KING DAVID KALAKAUA...Honolulu
JOHN OWEN DOMINIS..	"
WILLIAM COOPER PARKE...	"
GEORGE WILLIAMS	(4)...	"

ILLINOIS.
FRANCIS A. HAYDEN	(1)...Chicago

IOWA.
GEORGE WASHINGTON ASHTON......................................Lyons
GEORGE WASHINGTON PARKER......................................	"
ARTEMUS LAMB...Clinton

James Van Deventer..Clinton
George W. Bever..Cedar Rapids
James Morton   (6).. "   "

JAPAN.

Durham White Stevens...Tokio
Oscar Keil...Yokohama
Augustus Langfeldt...   "
Adolpho Farsari (4)...   "

KANSAS.

John Henry Brown...Wyandotte
John Calvin Carpenter.......... ....Leavenworth
Alonzo Cheney Emmons.....................................   "
Peter John Freling...   "
Burton Everington Langdon................................Fort Scott
Matthew Murray Miller.....................................Clay Center
Adrian Cyrus Sherman.........................,.............Rossville
Charles Spaulding...Topeka
Evan Davis... ....   "
Charles Stiles Wilder..Lawrence
Jeremiah Giles Smith..Wichita
Jeremiah Simpson Cole   (12).............................. "

KENTUCKY.

George C. Betts............................... ....Louisville
James Alexander Beattie................................. "
John William Cook.,.. "
John Finzer.. "
Henry Weeden Gray....................................... "
Edwin Gilbert Hall.. "
Henry Harrison Neal..... .... "
William Reinecke...............................,...•........... "
William Ryan... "
Levi Sloss... "
Kilbourne Walter Smith.............................. ... "
Charles Christopher Vogt................................. "
Thomas Underwood Dudley................................ "
Frank H. Johnson (Deputy for Kentucky).................... "
Burton F. Langdon....................................... "
Charles H. Fisk..Covington
Robert Talbot Miller................................. .... "
Warren LaRue Thomas.................................Marysville .
Campbell H. Johnson....................................Henderson
Max J. Mack....................................Cincinnati, Ohio
James G. Shields (21)..............................New Albany, Ind.

LOUISIANA.

Albert G. Brice ....New Orleans
Emmett DeWitt Craig........................... "   "
Alfred Henry Isaacson....................................... "   "

GEORGE SOULE...New Orleans
HENRY PEET BUCKLEY.. "   "
CHARLES E. KELLS.. "   "
ANDREW HERO, JR... "   "
JOSEPH POTTS HORNER.. "   "
THOMAS CRIPPS.. "   "
MARK QUAYLE   (10).. "   "

MARYLAND.

THOMAS AUGUSTUS CUNNINGHAM.............................Baltimore
JOHN HAZLEHURST BONNEVILLE LATROBE........................... "
NATHAN LEHMAN... "
CHARLES THOMAS SISCO... "
DAVID WEISENFIELD... "
THOMAS JACOB SHRYOCK   (6).................................. "

MINNESOTA.

GILES WILLIAM MERRILL....................................St. Paul
ORVILLE GILBERT MILLER.. "
CHARLES WHIPPLE NASH... "
JOHN CARL TERRY... "
CALEB HENRY BENTON...................................Minneapolis
EDWARD ARMENIUS HOTCHKINS..................................... "
JAMES MONTGOMERY WILLIAMS.................................... "
DAVID MARCUS GOODWIN... "
JOSEPH HAYES THOMPSON....................................... "
SAMUEL S. KILVINTON   (10)................................. "

MISSOURI.

AMBROSE WEBSTER FREEMAN....................................St. Louis
THOMAS ELWOOD GARRETT .... "
WILLIAM NAPOLEON LOKER...................................... "
STEPHEN BROWN POTTER....................................... "
STEPHEN D. THACHER   (5).............................Kansas City

MISSISSIPPI.

FREDERICK SPEED   (1)................................Vicksburg

MONTANA.

HARRY RETZER COMBY..Helena
CORNELIUS HEDGES.. "
JOHN CRITTENDEN MAJOR   (3)................................. "

NEBRASKA.

HARRY PORTER DEUEL....................................Omaha
ELBERT FREEMAN DUKE.. "
JOHN JAMES MONELL, JR...................................... "
CHARLES PHILIP NEEDHAM..................................... "
ROBERT HENRY HALL... "
WILLIAM CLEBURNE.. "
HENRY CLAY AKIN... "
ROBERT HECTOR OAKLEY..................................Lincoln
EDGAR SWARTWOUT DUDLEY.................................... "

THOMAS SEWELL...Lincoln
ROBERT WILKINSON FURNAS.............. ....Brownsville
BENJAMIN FRANKLIN RAWALT....................................Hastings
JAMES ALLEN TULLEYS..Red Cloud
EDWIN FORCE WARREN...................................... Nebraska City
FRANK HENRY YOUNG (15)..Custer

NEVADA.
FLETCHER HARRIS HARMON (1)..............................Eureka

NEW YORK.
JOSEPH THOMAS BROWN (1)...............................New York City

NORTH DAKOTA.
ANDREW HORACE BURKE.....................................Fargo
MARK ANTHONY BREWER.....................................	"
CHARLES CHRISTIAN KNEISLEY...........................	"
THOMAS CHASE PAXTON......................................	"
FRANK JURED THOMPSON.....................................	"
DANIEL FRANK ETTER (6).....................................Yankton

OREGON.
STEPHEN FOWLER CHADWICK...................................Salem
CHRISTOPHER TAYLOR.................... ....Dayton
JOSEPH NORTON DOLPH........................ ....Portland
JOHN R. FOSTER...	"
IRVING W. PRATT...	"
FERDINAND N. SHURTLIFF (6)...............................	"

SOUTH CAROLINA.
JOHN SOMERS BUIST..Charleston
JOHN FREDERICK FICKEN..................................	"
HENRY WHARTENBERG SHRÖDER...........................	"
THOMAS MOULTRIE MORDECAI (4)............................	"

TENNESSEE.
FORDYCE FOSTER BOWEN.................................. ....Memphis
JOHN ZENT..	"
CHARLES HAZEN EASTMAN....................................Nashville
JOHN FRIZZELL..	"
PITKIN C. WRIGHT...	"
EUGENE HERMAN PLUMACHER..................................	"
BENJAMIN RUFUS HARRIS..................................Jackson
HENRY R. HOWARD (8).......................................Tullahoma

TEXAS.
JOSEPH KNIGHT ASHBY...................................... Fort Worth
SPOTSWOOD WELLFORD LOMAX............................	"	"
SIDNEY MARTIN..	"	"
AUSTIN BEVERLY CHAMBERLIN...............................Sabine Pass
CHARLES SOLOMON MORSE.................. ....Austin
LOUIS MONTCALM OPENHEIMER........................ ....Calvert
NAHOR BRIGGS YARD...Galveston
RUDOLPH GRIMMER (8)......................................Dallas

VIRGINIA.

CHARLES ALBERT NESBITT..Richmond
HENRY FLOOD BOCOCK.......................................Lynchburg
EDWARD ADDISON CRAIGHILL.............................. "
WILLIAM LURAY PAGE .... "
FREDERICK GREENWOOD.......................................Norfolk
DANIEL JAMES TURNER (6)....................................Portsmouth

WEST VIRGINIA.

WILLIAM J. APPLEGATE.......................................Wellsburg
KEPHART DELWAR WALKER..................................Fairmount
JOHN WILLIAM MORRIS.......................................Wheeling
THOMAS MILLIGAN DARRAH (4).......................... "

WASHINGTON.

THOMAS MILBURNE REED.......................................Olympia
ROSSELL GALBRAITH O'BRIEN.............................. "
JOSEPH AUGUSTUS KUHN.......................................Port Townsend
JAMES M. BUCKLEY.......................................New Tacoma
WILLIAM PARKHURST WINANS ....Walla Walla
MARSHALL WILLIAM WOOD, U. S. A...............Fort Walla Walla
LOUIS ZEIGLER (7)....................................Spokane Falls

WYOMING.

ASAHEL COLLINS BECKWITH.......................................Evanston
FRANK MILLS FOOTE, Deputy.............................. "
JESSE KNIGHT (3)....................................... "

Total Honorary Members, 205.

Emeriti Honorary Members.

There are Forty-three Emeriti Honorary Members who belong to the Northern and to the Foreign Supreme Councils of the World.

———o———

Court of Honor.

Knights Grand Crosses Honorary 33d Degree.

STEPHEN HENRY BEASELY.......................................Alabama
ISAAC SUTVENE TITUS ....San Francisco, Cal.
GEORGE JOHN HOBE .... " " "
ELISHA INGRAHAM BAILEY, U. S. Army.............. " " "
JOSEPH THOMAS BROWN.......................Washington, D. C.
CLEMENT WELLS BENNETT.............................. " "
LUTHER HAMILTON PIKE .... " "
WILLIAM REYNOLDS SINGLETON .... "
KING DAVID KALAKAUA ....Honolulu, H. I.
GOVERNOR JOHN OWEN DOMINIS.............................. " "
JOHN WILLIAM COOK ....Louisville, Ken.
JOHN FRAZIER HEAD, U. S. Army.............................. " "
WILLIAM REINECKE .... " "

EDWIN GILBERT HALL	Louisville, Ken.
WILLIAM RYAN	" "
THOMAS CRIPPS	New Orleans, La.
THOMAS ELWOOD GARRETT	St. Louis, Mo.
WILLIAM NAPOLEON LOKER	" "
ORNILLE GILBERT MILLER	St. Paul, Minn.
GEORGE C. BETTS	Nebraska
ROBERT WILKINSON FURNAS	Brownsville, "
STEPHEN FOWLER CHADWICK	Salem, Oregon
ROCKY PRETSON EARHART	Portland, "
JOHN SOMERS BUIST	Charleston, S. C.
ABRAHAM EPHRAIM FRANKLAND	Memphis, Tenn.
WILLIAM LURAY PAGE	Lynchburg, Virginia
HARVEY ALLEN OLNEY	" "
EDWARD ADDISON CRAIGHILL	" "
FREDERICK GREENWOOD	Norfolk, "
KEPHART DELWAR WALKER	Fairmount, W. Va.
JOSEPH KNIGHT ASHBY	Fort Worth, Texas

Knights Grand Crosses of the 32d Degree.

JOSHUA OTIS STANTON 32°	Washington, D. C.
JOHN FOX DAMON, 32°	Seattle, State of Washington

Knights Commanders of the Court of Honor.

(Masters of the Royal Secret 32ds not 33ds.)

ALABAMA.

WALTER LAWRENCE BRAGG	Montgomery
DAVID CLOPTON	"
JAMES T. PIERCE	Warrior
JOHN WALTER TOMLINSON	Birmingham
SAMUEL TANNER BUTTLE	"
RUDOLPH MESTIER MULFORD (5)	"

ARIZONA.

MARTIN W. KALES (1)	Phœnix

CALIFORNIA.

HARRY HOLLES	San Francisco
WILLIAM SCHUYLER MOSES	"
AARON JONATHAN MESSING	"
WILLIAM A. ROBERTSON	"
SAMUEL W. ROSENSTOCK	"
JOHN HENRY TITCOMB	"
BERNARD FRANZ	"
REUBEN HEDLEY LLOYD	"
CHARLES HENRY WELLS	"
HENRY WOLFSOHN	"
STEPHEN WING	"
SAMUEL WOLF LEVY	"

CHARLES FRANKLIN BURNHAM.. Oakland
GEORGE PATTERSON... "
CHARLES DEXTER PIERCE... "
WILLIAM CALDWELL BELCHER.............................Marysville
THOMAS HUGH KERNAN .... "
HENRY SAYRE ORME..Los Angeles
ISADORE E. COHN... "
JAMES ROBERT DUPUY (33° elect)............................ "
CHARLES WESLEY LONG...................................Eureka

DISTRICT OF COLUMBIA.

GEORGE MILTON BARKER.............................Washington City
GEORGE W. BALLOCH...................................... "
GEORGE EDGAR CORSON.............................. .... "
HENRY LOUD CRAWFORD.................................. "
CHARLES COLTON DUNCANSON............................. . "
ALEXANDER H. HOLT...................................... "
JAMES LANSBURGH.. "
ALONZO JOEL MARSH..................................... "
GEORGE ENOCH NOYES................................... "
ISAAC PITTMAN NOYES................................... "
LEROY MORTIMER TAYLOR (11)........................... "

FLORIDA.

ROBERT JUDSON PERRY (1)................................Key Wes

GEORGIA.

CHARLES H. GOODRICH......................................Augusta
CHARLES W. HARRIS..................................... "
SAMUEL LAWRENCE.......................................Atlanta
CHARLES LEONARD WILSON............................... "
HENRY CLAY STOCKDELL (5)............................. "

IDAHO.

NEWELL JONATHAN BROWN..............................Hawley
HENRY BEWS (2)....................................... "

IOWA.

THERON ROMEYN BEERS...................................Lyons
WILLIAM WILBURN SANBORN.............................. "
CHARLES W. WARNER................................... "
GEORGE M. CURTIS............ ....Clinton
JAMES SCOTT JENKINS................................. "
ERASTUS A. WADLEIGH................................. "
NEWTON R. PARVIN...................................Cedar Rapids
UPTON C. BLAKE...................................... "
CALVIN GRAVES GREEN............................... "
CYRUS WALDCRAVE EATON............................. "
EDWARD C. AINSWOTH................................Des Moines

JAPAN.

STUART ELDRIDGE...Yokohama
ANDREW PATTERSON............................ .... "
CONSTANT WILLIAM DIMOCK...Kobi
ROBERT HUGHES.. "

KANSAS.

DAVID PASSON ....Lawrence
JUSTUS ASSMAN.. "
JAMES F. BAYLES.. "
EDWARD VAN BUREN.. "
ALBIN WEBER.. "
REUBEN H. HERSHFIELD.. "
JOSEPH WILKINS PARK.. "
JOHN WESTLAKE.. "
LUKE MICHAEL HAVENS..Fort Scott
ARTHUR CHARLES PERRY... "   "
WALTER WHITE PHILL''S.......................................,.Topeka
THEOPHILUS PATTERSON ROGERS................................ "
JOHN WHERRELL.. ....Paola
HARPER SAMUEL CUNNINGHAM................................Salina
EDWARD C. CULP (15).. "

KENTUCKY.

HENRY CADWALADER ADAMS, stationed at.................Philadelphia, Pa
JAMES ANDREWS BURRELL...Louisville
HENRY L. BURKHARDT.. "   •
RICHARD B. CALDWELL.................... .... "
JOHN V. COWLING... "
JOHN WINFIELD HAMMOND..................................... "
HENRY HUDSON... "
HORACE JANUARY.. "
WILLIAM HENRY MEFFERT...................................... "
THEOPHILUS STERN... "
HENRY GOLDMAN STEIBEL...................................... "
DAVID HUNTER WILSON... "
GEORGE T. EVANS... "
HENRY B. GRANT... "
WILLIAM R. JOHNSON.. "
GEORGE KOPMEIER.. "
HENRY BOSTWICK...Covington
ROBERT T. MILLER.. "
JAMES W. STATON..Brooksville
JOHN WILLIAM PRUELL..............................   Frankfort
THOMAS ELWOOD LEVIZEY (21)................... .....Newport

LOUISIANA.

RUDOLPH H. BENNERS..New Orleans
WILLIAM TORBETT BENEDICT.................................. "   " .
BIANCO CAMPEGLIO.. "   "

HENRY WALTER COULTER...New Orleans
WILLIAM R. DOUGLAS.. " "
JOSEPH HENRY DE GRANGE.. .... " "
GEORGE B. ITTMAN....................................... " "
CARLOS MADUEL.. " "
JOHN O. McLEAN.. " "
GEORGE MINIERI.. " "
CHARLES WESLEY NEWTON........................... ...... " "
JEAN BAPTISTE SORAPURN. .... " "
JOHN ALEXANDER STEVENSON.. " "
FRANCISCO PAULA DE VILLESANA............................. " "
JOSEPH VOEGTLE.. " "
EDWARD A. YORK.. " "
JOHN WILLIAM HADDEN.. " "
RICHARD LAMBERT.. " "
CHARLES F. BUCK.. " "
PAUL M. SCHNEIDER.. " "
DAVID ARENT...Farmersville
ABEL J. NORWOOD...... (22).......................................Clinton

MARYLAND.

WILLIAM FRANCIS COCKRAN..Baltimore
HERMAN L. EMMONS.. "
JACOB EMERY KEREBS.. "
MAURICE LANPHEIMER.. "
HENRY CLAY LARRABEE (5).. "

MINNESOTA.

ROBERT S. ALDEN...St. Paul
GEORGE HUNSAKER.. "
DELOS A. MONFORT.. "
NEWTON IRVINE WILLEY... "
WILLIAM HENRY STERLING WRIGHT.................................. "
GEORGE REUBEN METCALF.. "
WILLIAM MINER BUSHNELL.. "
WILLIAM PARKER JEWETT... "
EDWARD HENRY MILHAM...St. Paul
JOHN WALWORTH HENION....,.................................Minneapolis
ALBERT ENOS HIGBEE.. "
JOHN ALBERT SCHLENER.. "
DAVID MARCUS GOODWIN................................:.............. "
HENRY ROCKWOOD DENNY...Carver
SILAS BUCK FOOTE..Red Wing
SWANTE JOHN WILLARD .... "
REV. GEORGE B. WHIPPLE..Faribault
THOMAS MONTGOMERY... ......St. Peter
CLARK HORTON PORTER..Winona
DOUGLAS RUDD SUTHERLAND.......................................Monis
ROYAL HATCH GOVE (21)...Rochester

MISSOURI.

JOHN HENRY DEEMS..St. Louis
WILLIAM DOUGLAS.. "
JOHN R. PARSONS... "
HIRAM HENRY STEIBEL .... "
WILLIAM PARSONS MOORE (5).. '

MONTANA.

HENRY H. GURTHRIE..Helena
JAMES H. MOE.. "
ANTHONY HUNDLEY BARRETT....................................Butte
JOSEPH ANTHONY HYDE.. '
ROBERT C. KNOX.. "
WILLIAM THOMPSON (6)... "

NEBRASKA.

GUSTAV ANDERSON...Omaha
FRED JAMES BUTHWICK.. "
CARL AUGUSTUS FRIED... "
CHARLES SMITH HUNTINGTON...................................... "
FREDERICK BROWN LOWE.. "
GEORGE MURRAY NATTINGER... "
JOHN GILBERT TAYLOR.. "
CHARLES RICE TURNEY.. "
CHARLES MAY CARTER...Lincoln
CHARLES H. WILLARD...
EDWIN CATLIN WEBSTER (11).....................................Hastings

NEVADA.

HENRY W. BOLLEN..Carson City
FRED DAN STADTMULLER... "
GEORGE BUSH HILL.. "
GEORGE TUXFLY.. "
ALEXANDER FRASER...Eureka
DAVID HENRY HALL... "
JOHN EDWARD JONES.. "
HIRAM JOHNSON.. "
REINHOLD SADLER.. "
PEPI STELER.. "
THOMAS WREN.. "
GIOVANNI TORRE (12).. "

NORTH CAROLINA.

MICHAEL BOWERS..Raleigh
FABIUS HAYWARD BUSBEE... "
HENRY THEODORE BOHNSON (3)......................................Salem

NORTH DAKOTA.

WILLIAM ADDISON BENTLY...Bismark
ANDREW HORACE BURKE...Fargo
ERNEST J. SCHWELLENBACK.....................................Jonestown

WILLIAM BLATT...Yankton
LEVI BUTLER FRENCH..   "
GEORGE A. ARCHER...   "
ALBERT BREWER GUPTIL..Fargo
SAMUEL THOMAS CORMICK..   "
JOSEPH SELDEN HUNTINGTON...   "
JAMES TWAMLEY...   "
OSCAR S. GIFFORD (11)..Sioux Falls

NEW MEXICO.
WILLIAM WASHINGTON GRIFFIN..Santa Fe

OREGON.
JAMES R. BAYLEY...Newport
HENRY C. MORRICE..Portland
SETH L. POPE..   "
ANDREW ROBERTS..   "
BENJAMIN GARDNER WHITEHOUSE (4)...............................   "

SOUTH CAROLINA.
ISAAC WAYNE ANGEL..Charleston
ERRINGTON BROWN HUME...   "
ALEXANDER WASHINGTON MARSHALL.................................   "
W. JAMES WHALEY (4)...   "

TENNESSEE.
HENRY MARTIN AIKEN..Knoxville
ROGER EASTMAN..Nashville
WILLIAM AUSTIN SMITH (3)...Columbia

TEXAS.
WILLIAM MORGAN ANDREWS...Galveston
BENJAMIN FOLGER DISBROW...   "
BENJAMIN LeCOMPTE...   "
WILLIAM SCRIMGEOUR...   "
BENJAMIN OVERFIELD HAMILTON......................................   "
FRANK DURANG HARRAR..   "
SYMON CONRADI...   "
HENRY LINCOLN CARLTON...Austin
JOHN McDONALD..   "
GEORGE MELLERSH..   "
TOM MURRAH...   "
JOHN C. McCOY..Dallas
CHARLES ALBERT HOTCHKISS...   "
ROBERT BREWSTER...Houston
STEPHEN DECATUR MOORE..   "
PIERRE LEON QUERONZE..   "
HENRY SHERFFINS..   "
JAMES SHEPHERD SULLIVAN...Richmon
CHARLES BENJAMIN PATRICK...El Paso
HENRY ADDINGTON GILPIN...Collins
SYMON ROSENFIELD (21)..Fort Worth

VIRGINIA.

JAMES GASKINS BAIN..................:.......................................Portsmouth
STEPHEN MCGEE FISHER...Richmond
DAVID HUSTED..Lynchburg
THOMAS E. MOORMAN............................... ....   "
DINWIDDIE B. PHILLIPS..…..........   "
JOHN R. SPILLMAN...   "
JOHN J. TERRILL..   "
SAMUEL TYLER...   "
ABRAHAM MYERS   (9)..Norfolk

WEST VIRGINIA.

JACOB BERGER...Wheeling
JEREMIAH A. MILLER   (2)...   "

WASHINGTON.

ALEXANDER FAY ANDERSON..Seattle
WILLIAM HENRY GILLIAM...   "
GRANVILLE OWEN HALLER...   "
EDWARD STURGIS INGRAHAM.......................................   "
CHARLES ALBERT WRIGHT...   "
JOHN JACOB GILBERT...Olympia
JOHN FRANKLIN GOWEY...   "
WILLIAM MCMICKEN............................ ....   "
NATHAN SMITH PORTER..   "
JOHN WHITE EDWARDS...Port Blakely
FRANCIS TARBELL...…........Tacoma
WALTER JAMES THOMPSON..:...   "
CYRUS WALKER, Port Gamble...   "
LEVI ANKENEY...Walla Walla
RALPH GUICHARD.. "   "
JAMES HEWITT SMITH   (16)......... .... "   "

REGISTER OF SUBORDINATE BODIES

OF THE

Supreme Council of the Thirty-Third Degree

OF THE

Ancient and Accepted Scottish Rite of Freemasonry for the Southern Jurisdiction of the United States, 1890.

Grand Consistories, 31° and 32°:

1 CALIFORNIA..San Francisco, Cal.
2 EMPIRE OF JAPAN...Yokohama, Japan
3 KENTUCKY............. ....Louisville, Kentucky.
4 LOUISIANA...New Orleans, La

NOTE.—These Grand Consistories are the local Grand Bodies for the government of the Councils of Kadosh, Chapters of Rose Croix and Lodges of Perfection for their local jurisdictions and also confer the 31st and 32d Degrees.

Consistories, 31°–32°.

1   ALBERT PIKE, No. 1.......................Washington City, D. C.
2   DAKOTA, No. 1...............................Fargo, North Dakota
3   AUGUSTA, No. 1..............................Augusta, Georgia
4   DE MOLAY, No. 1.................................Lyons, Iowa
5   IOWA, No. 2......................................Cedar Rapids, "
6   LEAVENWORTH, No. 1.......................Leavenworth, Kansas
7   WICHITA, No. 2..................................Wichita,   "
8   CHESAPEAKE, No. 1........................Baltimore, Maryland
9   OCCIDENTAL, No. 1...........................Omaha, Nebraska
10 MISSOURI, No. 1..............................St. Louis, Missouri
11 MINNESOTA, No. 1............................St. Paul, Minnesota
12 MINNEAPOLIS, No. 2......................Minneapolis,   "
13 LAWSON, No. 1..............................Seattle, State of Wash.
14 FORT WORTH, No. 1.......................Forth Worth, Texas
15 BIRMINGHAM, No. 1.......................Birmingham, Alabama
16 OCCIDENTAL——............................Los Angeles, California
17 COLORADO, No. 1..............................Denver, Colorado
18 ZAREPTHAII——.............................Davenport, Iowa

Councils or Preceptories of Kadosh, 19°–80°.

1   EAGLE, No. 6...New Orleans, Louisiana
2   LOS AMIGOS DEL ORDEN, No. 7.................   "   "   "
3   FOYER MACONNIQUE, No. 8.....................   "   "   "
4   KILWINNING, No. 1.................................Louisville, Kentucky
5   GODFREY DE ST. OMAR, No. 1.........................San Francisco, Cal
6   DE MOLAY, No. 2.....................................Oakland,   "
7   HUGO DES PAYENS, No. 3...........................Los Angeles,   "
8   MULTNOMAH, No. 1...............................Portland, Oregon
9   WASHINGTON, No. 1.............................Seattle, State of Wash.
10 DE MOLAI, No. 2.................................Olympia, "   "   "
11 ROBERT DE BRUCE, No. 1.....................Washington City, D. C.
12 ALEXANDER LIHOLIHO, No. 1.........................Honolulu, H. I.
13 HUGH DES PAYENS, No. 1...............................Lyons, Iowa
14 ST. ANDREWS, No. 2.................................Cedar Rapids,   "
15 CŒUR DE LION——...................................Davenport,   "
16 DES PAYENS....................................Yokohama, Japan
17 DE MOLAI——....................................Leavenworth, Kansas
18 WILLIAM DE LA MORE, No. 1...........................Lawrence,   "
19 GODFREY DE ST. OMAR——..........................Topeka,   "
20 ROBERT DE BRUCE, No. 4.............................Fort Scott,   "
21 MARYLAND, No. 1.................................Baltimore, Maryland
22 DE MOLAI, No. 1....................................St. Paul, Minnesota
23 ALFRED ELISHA AMES, No. 2.....................Minneapolis,   "
24 MISSOURI, No. 1.................................St. Louis, Missouri
25 ST. ANDREWS, No. 1.............................Omaha, Nebraska
26 ORIENT, No. 1....................................Austin, Texas
27 OLEANDER, No. 2...................................Galveston,   "
28 SIDNEY MARTIN, No. 3.............................Fort Worth,   "
29 DENVER, No. 1....................................Denver, Colorado
30 FARGO, No. 1....................................Fargo, North Dakota
31 ROBERT DE BRUCE, No. 2.................Yankton, North Dakota
32 CŒUR DE LEON, No. 3.................Sioux Falls,   "   "
33 WICHITA....................................Wichita, Kansas
34 SALINA.......................................Salina,   "
35 GILBERT DE LACY, No. 1.........................Birmingham, Alabama

Chapters of Rose Croix, 15°–18°.

1   BUIST, No. 1...Charleston, South Carolina
2   PELICAN, No. 11......................................New Orleans, Louisana
3   CERVANTES, No. 5.....................................   "   "
4   FOYER MACONNIQUE, No. 6........................   "   "
5   PELICAN, No. 1.................................Louisville, Kentucky
6   COVINGTON, No. 2.................................Covington, Kentucky
7   YERBA BUENA, No. 4.............................San Francisco, California
8   GETHSEMANE, No. 5.................................Oakland,   "
9   ROBERT BRUCE, No. 6.............................Los Angeles,   "

10	DAI NIPPON, No. 1	Yokohama, Japan
11	EVANGELIST, No. 1	Washington City, D. C.
12	MACKEY, No. 1	Denver, Colorado
13	MACKEY, No. 1	Yankton, Dakota
14	PELICAN, No. 2	Fargo, North Dakota
15	TEMPLE, No. 1	Savannah, Georgia
16	NUUANU, No. 1	Honolulu, Hawaiian Islands
17	DELPHIC, No. 1	Lyons, Iowa
18	BRUCE, No. 2	Cedar Rapids, "
19	LEBANON, No. 3	Davenport, "
20	DAI NIPPON, No. 1	Yokohama, Japan
21	UNITY, No. 1	Topeka, Kansas
22	EQUALITY, No. 2	Lawrence "
23	DELTA, No. 3	Leavenworth "
24	MACKEY, No. 4	Fort Scott "
25	MEREDITH, No. 1	Baltimore, Maryland
26	ST. PAUL, No. 1	St. Paul, Minnesota
27	ST. VINCENT DE PAUL, No. 2	Minneapolis, "
28	ST. LOUIS, No. 1	St. Louis, Missouri
29	HELENA, No. 1	Helena, Montana
30	SEMPER FIDELIS, No. 1	Omaha, Nebraska
31	AINSWORTH, No. 1	Portland, Oregon
32	PHILIP C. TUCKER, No. 1	Austin, Texas
33	L. M. OPENHEIMER, No. 2	Galveston, "
34	S. W. LOMAX, No. 3	Fort Worth, "
35	EL PASO, No. 4	El Paso, "
36	ROPER, No. 2	Norfolk, Virginia
37	PELICAN, No. 3	Richmond, Virginia
38	CHARITY, No. 1	Wheeling, West Virginia
39	A. G. MACKEY, No. 1	Evanston, Wyoming
40	WASHINGTON, No. 1	Seattle, State of Washington
41	ROBERT BRUCE, No. 2	Olympia, " "
42	ST. ANDREWS, No. 3	Port Townsend, " "
43	ST. JOHNS, No. 4	Port Gamble, " "
44	COLUMBIA, No. 5	Walla Walla, " "
45	WICHITA, No. 5	Wichita, Kansas
46	SALINA, No. 6	Salina, "
47	MACKEY, No. 3	Red Wing, Minnesota
48	AREOPAGUS, No. 2	Kansas City, Missouri
49	EMANUEL, No. 2	Lincoln, Nebraska
50	CAPITOLIUM, No. 1	Carson City, Nevada
51	TEMPLE,	Savannah, Georgia
52	WHITE EAGLE	Atlanta, Georgia
53	CALVARY	Memphis, Tennessee
54	LIVINGSTON	Livingston, Montana
55	TACOMA	Tacoma, Washington
56	———	Spokane Falls, "
57	———	Duluth, Minnesota

𝔏𝔬𝔡𝔤𝔢𝔰 𝔬𝔣 𝔓𝔢𝔯𝔣𝔢𝔠𝔱𝔦𝔬𝔫, 4°--14°.

1	DELTA, No. 1	Charleston, South Carolina
2	ALBERT PIKE, No. 1	New Orleans, Louisiana
3	FOYER MACONNIQUE, No. 3	" "
4	CERVANTES, No. 5	" "
5	UNION, No. 3	Louisville, Kentucky
6	COVINGTON, No. 4	Covington, "
7	PACIFIC, No. 2	Marysville, California
8	YERBA BUENA, No. 6	San Francisco, "
9	HARTLEY, No. 7	Stockton, "
10	MYRTLE, No. 10	Eureka, "
11	OAKLAND, No. 12	Oakland, "
12	KING SOLOMON, No. 14	Los Angeles, "
13	SAN DIEGO, No. 15	San Diego, "
14	DAI NIPPON, No. 1	Yokohama, Japan
15	SANTA RITA, No. 1	Tucson, Arizona
16	ALABAMA, No. 1	Montgomery, Alabama
17	BIRMINGHAM, No. 2	Birmingham, "
18	MITHRAS, No. 1	Washington City, D. C.
19	ORIENT, No. 2	Georgetown, "
20	ALPHA, No. 1	Yankton, Dakota
21	ENOCH, No. 3	Fargo, North Dakota
22	KHURUM, No. 3	Sioux Falls, Dakota
23	WEBSTER, No. 4	Webster, "
24	CYRUS, No. 5	Watertown, "
25	ST. JOHNS, No. 1	Jacksonville, Florida
26	DEWITT C. DAWKINS, No. 2	Key West, "
27	ENOCH No. 1	Augusta, Georgia
28	EMETH, No. 2	Albany, "
29	ZERBAL, No. 3	Macon, "
30	HERMES, No. 4	Atlanta, "
31	EPSILON, No. 5	Savannah, "
32	KAMEHAMEHA, No. 1	Honolulu, Hawaiian Islands
33	IOWA, No. 1	Lyons, Iowa
34	KILWINNING, No. 2	Cedar Rapids, "
35	COVENANT, No. 1	Lewiston, Idaho
36	ELEUSIS, No. 1	Leavenworth, Kansas
37	ORIENTAL, No. 3	Topeka, "
38	VALLEY, No. 4	Clay Center, "
39	ZERBAL, No. 5	Lawrence, "
40	JOABERT, No. 6	Fort Scott, "
41	KHURUM, No. 7	Emporia, "
42	MACKEY, No. 8	Salina, "
43	ELMO, No. 9	Wichita, "
44	ALBERT PIKE, No. 1	Baltimore, Maryland
45	CARMEL, No. 1	St. Paul, Minnesota
46	EXCELSIOR, No. 2	Minneapolis, "

47	HARMONY, No. 3	Red Wing, Minnesota
48	OSIRIS, No. 4	Mankato, "
49	DELTA, No. 5	St. Peter, "
50	QUITMAN, No. 1	Vicksburg, Mississippi
51	ST. LOUIS, No. 1	St. Louis, Missouri
52	ALPHA, No. 2	Hannibal, "
53	ADONIRAM, No. 3	Kansas City, "
54	ALPHA, No. 1	Helena, Montana
55	BETA No. 2	Butte, "
56	DOUGLAS, No. 3	Granite, "
57	KHURUM, No. 4	Livingston, "
58	KILWINNING, No. 1	Grand Island, Nebraska
59	MOUNT MORIAH, No. 2	Omaha, "
60	FIDUCIA, No. 3	Hastings, "
61	DELTA, No. 4	Lincoln, "
62	NEVADA, No. 3	Carson City, Nevada
63	SANTA FE, No. 1	Santa Fe, New Mexico
64	OREGON, No. 1	Portland, Oregon
65	ALBERT PIKE, No. 2	Salem, "
66	JOHN CHESTER, No. 1	Jackson, Tennessee
67	EMETH, No. 2	Columbia, "
68	EMULATION, No. 3	Nashville, "
69	SINAI, No. 4	Murfreesboro, "
70	MIZPAH, No. 5	Memphis. "
71	SAN FILIPE, No. 1	Galveston, Texas
72	PALESTINE, No. 2	Palestine, "
73	FORT WORTH, No. 3	Fort Worth, "
74	FIDELITY, No. 4	Austin, "
75	EL PASO, No. 5	El Paso, "
76	SAN JACINTO, No. 6.	Houston "
77	ALBERT PIKE, No. 1	Lynchburg, Virginia
78	McDANIEL, No. 3	Norfolk, "
79	A. G. MACKEY, No. 4	Deep Creek, "
80	JOHN L. ROPER, No. 5	Richmond, "
81	PORTSMOUTH, No. 6	Portsmouth, "
82	McDANIEL, No. 1	Wheeling, West Virginia
83	WASHINGTON, No. 1	Seattle, State of Washington
84	OLYMPIA, No. 2	Olympia, " "
85	LA FAYETTE, No. 3	Port Townsend, " "
86	LEBANON, No. 4	Port Gamble, " "
87	COLUMBIA, No. 5	Walla Walla, " "
88	BAINBRIDGE, No. 6	Port Blakely, " "
89	DAYTON, No. 7	Dayton, " "
90	MACKEY, No. 8	Spokane Falls, " "
91	TACOMA, No. 9	Tacoma, " "
92	JORDAN, No. 1	Rawlins, Wyoming Ty.
93	ALBERT PIKE, No. 2	Evanston, "

TABLEAU

OF THE

Supreme Council of Sovereign Grand Inspectors-General

OF THE THIRTY-THIRD AND LAST DEGREE,

FOR THE

Northern Masonic Jurisdiction of the United States of America.

GRAND EAST, BOSTON, MASSACHUSETTS.

1889-1890.

Officers.

1 HENRY L. PALMER, Milwaukee, Wis., *M. P. Sov. Grand Commander*
2 CHARLES LEVI WOODBURY, Boston, Mass., *P. Grand Lieut.* "
3 SAMUEL CROCKER LAWRENCE, Boston, Mass., *Grand Min. of State*
4 MARQUIS F. KING, Portland, Me., *Deputy for Maine*
5 FRANK A. McKEAN, Nashua, N. H., " *New Hampshire*
6 GEORGE O. TYLER, Burlington, Vt., " *Vermont*
7 BENJAMIN DEAN, Boston, Mass., " *Massachusetts*
8 NEWTON D. ARNOLD, Providence, R. I., " *Rhode Island*
9 CHARLES WILLIAM CARTER, Norwich, Conn., " *Connecticut*
10 JOHN HODGE, Lockport, N. Y., " *New York*
11 ANDREW B. FRAZEE, Camden, N. J., " *New Jersey*
12 ANTHONY E. STOCKER, Philadelphia, Pa., " *Pennsylvania*
13 HUGH McCURDY, Corunna, Mich., " *Michigan*
14 ENOCH TERRY CARSON, Cincinnati, O., " *Ohio*
15 NICHOLAS R. RUCKLE, Indianapolis, Ind., " *Indiana*
16 JOHN CORSON SMITH, Chicago, Ill., " *Illinois*
17 ALBERT V. H. CARPENTER, Milwaukee, Wis., " *Wisconsin*
18 HEMAN ELY, Elyria, Ohio, *Grand Treasurer General*
19 CLINTON FREEMAN PAIGE, Binghampton, N. Y.,
Grand Secretary General
20 LUCIUS R. PAIGE, Cambridgeport, Mass., *Grand Keeper of Archives*
21 CHARLES T. McCLENACHAN, New York City, N. Y.,
Grand Master of Ceremonies

22	ROBERT EMMETT PATTERSON,	*Grand Marshal General*
23	WILLIAM R. HIGBY,	*Grand Standard Bearer*
24	GEORGE OTIS TYLER,	*Grand Captain of the Guard*

25 ALBERT P. MORIARTY, Hon. 33°, New York City, N. Y.,
Assistant Grand Secretary General

---

26 REV. JOSEPH LAFAYETTE SEWARD, Hon. 33°, Lowell, Mass.,
Grand Prior

27 J. H. HOBART WARD, Hon. 33°, New York City, N. Y.,
Grand Marshal of the Camp

28 OZIAS W. SHIPMAN, Hon. 33°, Detroit, Mich.,
Grand Marshal of the Camp

29 GILBERT W. BARNARD, Hon. 33°, Chicago, Ill.,
Grand Marshal of the Camp

30 ANDREW NEMBACH, Hon. 33°, Cincinnati, Ohio,   *Grand Organist*

Trustees of Permanent Fund.

1	BENJAMIN DEAN	Term expires 1890
2	JOHN L. STETTINIUS	" " 1891
3	SAMUEL C. LAWRENCE	" " 1892
4	ROBERT M. C. GRAHAM	" " 1893
5	CLINTON F. PAIGE	" " 1894
6	CHARLES L. WOODBURY	" " 1895
7	HENRY L. PALMER	" " 1896

Active Members.

1	JOHN CHRISTIE	Portsmouth, N. H.
2	DANIEL SICKLES	Brooklyn, N. Y.
3	LUCIUS ROBINSON PAIGE	Cambridgeport, Mass.
4	WILLIAM PARKMAN	Boston, Mass.
5	HOSMER ALLEN JOHNSON	Chicago, Ill.
6	ANTHONY EUGENE STOCKER	Philadelphia, Penn.
7	CHAS. T. McCLENACHAN	New York City, N. Y.
8	HENRY CHAPMAN BANKS	New York City. N. Y.
9	DAVID BURNHAM TRACY	Detroit, Mich.
10	JOSIAH H. DRUMMOND	Portland, Me.
11	BENJAMIN DEAN	Boston, Mass.
12	ENOCH T. CARSON	Cincinnati, Ohio
13	WILLIAM RILEY HIGBY	Bridgeport, Conn.
14	CLINTON F. PAIGE	Binghampton, N. Y.
15	GEORGE W. BENTLEY	New London, Conn.
16	HENRY L. PALMER	Milwaukee, Wis.
17	ROBERT HARRIS FOSS	Chicago, Ill.
18	HEMAN ELY	Elyria, Ohio
19	HOMER L. GOODWIN	Bethlehem, Penn.
20	CHARLES W. CARTER	Norwich, Conn.
21	JOHN CAVEN	Indianapolis, Ind.

22	ROBERT M. C. GRAHAM	New York City, N. Y.
23	SAMUEL C. LAWRENCE	Boston, Mass.
24	WALTER A. STEVENS	Chicago, Ill.
25	GEORGE O. TYLER	Burlington, Vt.
26	CHARLES BROWN	Cincinnati, Ohio
27	BRENTON D. BABCOCK	Cleveland, "
28	JOHN L. STETTINIUS	" "
29	CHARLES E. MYER	Philadelphia, Penn.
30	ROBERT E. PATTERSON	" "
31	ALBERT V. H. CARPENTER	Milwaukee, Wis.
32	NEWTON D. ARNOLD	Providence, R. I.
33	AUGUSTUS R. HALL	Philadelphia, Penn.
34	FRANK A. McKEAN	Nashua, N. H.
35	EDWARD P. BURNHAM	Saco, Me.
36	JOHN CORSON SMITH	Chicago, Ill.
37	ANDREW B. FRAZER	Camden, N. J.
38	HUGH McCURDY	Corrunna, Mich.
39	NICHOLAS R. RECKLE	Indianapolis, Ind.
40	CHARLES M. COTTRILL	Milwaukee, Wis.
41	FRANKLIN H. BASCOM	Montpelier, Vt.
42	MARQUIS F. KING	Portland, Me.
43	PHINEAS G. C. HUNT	Indianapolis, Ind.
44	GEORGE M. CARPENTER	Providence. R. I.
45	JOHN HODGE	Lockport, N. Y.
46	GEORGE W. CURRIER	Nashua, N. H.

Emeriti Members.

1	ATHANASIUS COLO VELONI	Brooklyn, N. Y.
2	FRANCIS A. BLADES	Detroit, Mich.

Honorary Members, 33°.

MAINE.

1 Joseph A. Locke, Portland,
2 Almon C. Waite, Portland,
3 Rufus H. Hinkley, "
4 Silas Alden, Bangor, •
5 Arlington B. Marston, Bangor,
6 Charles W. Belknap, Portland,
7 Stephen Berry, Portland,
8 John S. Russell, Portland,
9 Albro E. Chase, "
10 George R. Shaw, "
11 Samuel F. Bearce, "
12 Edmund B. Mallett Jr, Freeport,
13 Augustus B. Farnham, Bangor,
14 Albert M. Penley, Auburn,
15 William J. Burnham, Lewiston.

NEW HAMPSHIRE.

1 Thomas E. Hatch, Keene,
2 Henry B. Atherton, Nashua,
3 Joseph W. Fellows, Manchester,
4 John J. Bell, Exeter,
5 George B. Cleaves, Concord,
6 Andrew Bunton, Manchester,
7 John F. Webster, "
8 Joseph Shattuck, Nashua,
9 Charles H. Webster, Nashua,
10 Charles C. Danforth, Concord.

VERMONT.

1 Levi Underwood, Burlington,   2 Milton K. Paine, Windsor,
3 Fred'k F. Fletcher, St. Johnsbury, 4 William Brinsmaid, Burlington,
5 Marsh O. Perkins, Windsor,   6 Charles H. Heaton, Montpelier,
7 Myron W. Johnson, Burlington, 8 Howard H. Hill,   "
9 Fred'k L. Fisher, St. Johnsbury, 10 Albro F. Nichols, St. Johnsbury,
11 Warren G. Reynolds, Burlington, 12 George H. Kinsley, Burlington,
13 J. Henry Jackson, Bane,   14 Silas W. Cummings, St. Albans.

MASSACHUSETTS.

1 Nicholas Hathaway, Fall River,   2 Wm. F. Knowles, W. Somerville,
3 Daniel W. Lawrence, Medford,   4 Wyzeman Marshall, Boston,
5 Albert H. Kelsey, N. Cambridge, 6 James S. Freeland,   "
7 John K. Hall, Boston,   8 Charles C. Dume, Newburyport,
9 Edward A. White, Boston,   10 Benjamin F. Butler, Lowell,
11 William A. Smith,   "   12 William F. Salmon,   "
13 E. Dana Bancroft, Ayer,   14 Wm. A. Richardson, Cambridge,
15 Edward Stearns, Boston,   16 Thomas R. Lambert, Charlestown,
17 Samuel H. Gregory, Boston,   18 James A. Fox, Boston,
19 Percival L. Everett, Boston,   20 Sereno D. Nickerson, Boston,
21 Henry Mulliken,   "   22 George O. Carpenter,   "
23 William D. Stratton,   "   24 Benjamin A. Gould, Cambridge,
25 Henry Endicott, Cambridgeport, 26 William H. Cheesman, Boston,
27 William H. Guild, Boston,   28 Charles C. Hutchinson, Lowell,
29 Henry P. Perkins, Lowell,   30 Charles A. Welch, Boston,
31 Otis E. Weld, Boston,   32 John L. Stevenson,   "
33 William R. Alger, Boston,   34 Frederick G. Walbridge, Boston,
35 Edwin Wright,   "   36 Thomas Waterman,   "
37 Albert C. Smith,   "   38 C. H. Spellman, Springfield,
39 Samuel B. Spooner, Springfield, 40 Wm. J. Stevens, Kingston, N. H.
41 George S. Carpenter, Boston,   42 Erastus H. Doolittle, Boston,
43 E. Bentley Young,   "   44 Josiah C. Seward, Lowell,
45 Leonard M. Averill,   "   46 John H. Lakin, Boston,
47 G. B. Buckingham, Worcester, 48 Benjamin W. Rowell, Boston,
49 Minot J. Savage, Boston,   50 Joseph W. Work,   " .

RHODE ISLAND.

1 William B. Blanding, Providence, 2 Albert H. Chaffee, Worcester, Mass
3 James B. Brayton, Newport,   4 Eugene D. Burt, Providence,
5 Nicholas Van Sluyck, Providence 6 Stillman White, Providence.
7 Joseph O. Earle, Providence,   8 William J. Underwood, Newport,
9 George H. Kenyon, Providence.

CONNECTICUT.

1 Marcus C. Allen, Bridgeport,   2 Joseph K. Wheeler, Hartford,
3 Henry L. Parker, Norwich,   4 James L. Gould, Bridgeport,
5 Nathan A. Baldwin, Milford,   6 Charles E. Billings, Hartford,
7 Charles W. Skiff, Danbury,   8 Frederick H. Waldron, New Haven
9 William C. Seeley, Bridgeport, 10 Samuel M. Bronson, Hartford,
11 Arthur H. Brewer, Norwich,   12 Horatio G. Bronson, New Haven,
13 Elias S. Quintant, Bridgeport.

NEW YORK.

1 Henry S. Sloan, Binghampton,
2 Alfred Woodham, Brooklyn,
3 Albert P. Moriarty, Brooklyn,
4 John Vanderbeck, N. Y. City,
5 Robert Macoy, Brooklyn,
6 Gustavus W. Smith, N. Y. City,
7 William B. Newman, N. Y. City,
8 John A. Foster, N. Y. City,
9 Joseph J. Jennings, Brooklyn,
10 John Moon, Brooklyn,
11 Harrison S. Vining, Brooklyn,
12 J. H. Hobart Ward, N. Y. City,
13 Otis Cole, Rochester,
14 John R. Anderson, LeRoy,
15 John F. Collins, N. Y. City,
16 Henry J. Shields, Brooklyn,
17 George J. Gardner, Syracuse,
18 Seymour H. Stone, Syracuse,
19 Robert H. Waterman, Albany,
20 James W. Husted, Peekskill,
21 Edwin J. Loomis, Norwich,
22 John D. Williams, Elmira,
23 Edward A. Brown, Syracuse,
24 George Babcock, Troy,
25 Walter M. Fleming, N. Y. City,
26 Aaron L. Northrop, N. Y. City,
27 Charles Roome, N. Y. City,
28 John L. Sage, Rochester,
29 Jesse B. Anthony, Troy,
30 Samuel Jones, N. Y. City,
31 Benjamin F. Stiles, Skaneateles,
32 John C. Robinson, Binghampton,
33 Judson B. Andrews, Buffalo,
34 John S. Bartlett, Buffalo,
35 Abel G. Cook, Syracuse,
36 Augustus M. Koeth, Rochester,
37 James Ten Eyck, Albany,
38 George W. Gilbert, N. Y. City,
39 Jacob R. Telfair, Staten Island,
40 Edwin Gates, Brooklyn,
41 Edward M. L. Ehlers, N. Y. City,
42 Wm. L. Sage, Boston, Mass.,
43 William S. Patterson, N. Y. City,
44 John N. Macomb, Jr., Branchport
45 Augustus W. Peters, N. Y. City,
46 Herman H. Russ, Albany,
47 Charles W. Toney, Staten Island,
48 Joseph B. Eakins, N. Y. City,
49 William D. Garrison, N. Y. City,
50 Charles H. Heyser, N. Y. City,
51 Austin C. Wood, Syracuse,
52 Samuel C. Steele, Rochester,
53 Charles P. Clark, Syracuse,
54 John B. Thacher, Albany,
55 Hiram B. Berry, Warwick,
56 George W. Fuller, Corning,
57 Willard A. Pearce, N. Y. City,
58 Thomas Gliddon, Rochester,
59 Benj. Flagler, Susp'n Bridge,
60 William A. Brodie, Genessee,
61 George Wm. Millar, N. Y. City,
62 William J. Lawless, N. Y. City,
63 Albert Becker, Jr., Syracuse,
64 Foster Ely, Bridgefield, Conn.
65 Wayland Trask, Brooklyn,
66 Charles S. Ward, N. Y. City,
67 John W. Richardson, Brooklyn,
68 Joseph P. Abel, Brooklyn,
69 Richard H. Parker, Syracuse,
70 Frank R. Lawrence, N. Y. City,
71 Hiram W. Plumb, Syracuse,
72 James F. Ferguson, Cent'l. Valley
73 Edmund L. Judson, Albany,
74 William E. Fitch, Albany,
75 George McGown, Palmyra,
76 Simon V. McDowell, Rochester,
77 Edwin A. Thrall, Brooklyn,
78 Sydney F. Walker, Brooklyn,
79 James McGee, Brooklyn,
80 George H. Fitzwilson, N. Y. City,
81 George H. Clarke, Rochester,
82 Warren C. Hubbard, Brooklyn,
83 Edward F. Jones, Binghampton,
84 Byron S. Frisbie, Utica,
85 Frederic A. Benson, Bingh'pton
86 Daniel L. MacLellan, N. Y. City,
87 John F. Shafer, Menands, Alb'ny
88 Thomas R. Lombard, N. Y. City.

NEW JERSEY.

1 George Tucker, Hoboken,
2 G. B. Edwards, Jersey City H'ts,
3 Otis H. Tiffany, N. Y. City,
4 William W. Goodwin, Camden,
5 Charles Bechtel, Trenton,
6 M. Higginbotham, Jersey City,
7 George Scott, Paterson,
8 Jerome B. Borden, New Bruns'wck
9 George W. Steed, Camden,
10 Edward Mills, Camden.

PENNSYLVANIA.

1 Alex. M. Pollock, Pittsburg,
2 John Vallerchamp, Harrisburg,
3 Sydney Hayden, Athens,
4 Christian F. Knapp, Bloomsburg,
5 Isaac D. Lutz, Harrisburg,
6 Townsend S. Hunn, N. Y. City,
7 Chas. H. Kingston, Philadelphia,
8 Calvin L. Stowell, Rochester, N.Y.
9 Thomas R. Davis, Philadelphia,
10 Charles R. Earley, Ridgeway,
11 William H. Egle, Harrisburg,
12 Mark R. Muckle, Philadelphia,
13 Thomas R. Putton, Philadelphia,
14 John Sartain, Philadelphia,
15 Ed. S. Wyckoff, Philadelphia,
16 Henry Sartain, Philadelphia,
17 James H. Hopkins, Pittsburg,
18 George E. Ridgeway, Franklin,
19 James S. Barber, Pittsburg,
20 Benjamin B. Hill, St. Petersburg,
21 Charles W. Batchelor, Pittsburg,
22 DeWitt C. Carroll, Pittsburg,
23 Franklin Garrigues, Phila.,
24 George P. Balmain, Pittsburg,
25 Joseph Eichbaum, Pittsburg,
26 Samuel J. Dickey, Philadelphia,
27 Henry R. Coulomb, Phila.,
28 William B. Meredith, Kittanning,
29 John M. Clapp, Tidioute,
30 Eliphalet O. Lyte, Millersville,
31 George W. Guthrie, Pittsburg,
32 J. Frank Knight, Philadelphia,
33 Charles K. Francis, Phila.,
34 C. H. Cummings, Mauch Chunk,
35 B. E. Lehman, Bethlehem,
36 Edwin G. Martin, Allentown,
37 V. N. Shaffer, Phoenixville,
38 Joshua L. Lyte, Lancaster,
39 Samuel W. Wray, Philadelphia,
40 Matthias H. Henderson, Sharon,
41 W. H. Slack, Alleghany City,
42 James Kerr, Jr., Pittsburg,
43 John B. Arnold, Aurora, Ill.,
44 Joel S. Eaby, Lancaster,
45 Samuel B. Kennedy, Erie,
46 Charles C. Baer, Pittsburg,
47 Benjamin Darlington, Pittsburg,
48 Caleb C. Thompson, Warren.

OHIO.

1 John C. Bell, Cincinnati,
2 Wm. M. Cunningham, Newark,
3 George Hoadley, Cincinnati,
4 Charles A. Woodward, Cleveland,
5 Charles C. Keifer, Urbana,
6 James S. Totten, Lebanon,
7 Apollos M. Ross, Cincinnati,
8 Alex. B. Huston, Cincinnati,
9 Henry C. Urner, Cincinnati,
10 Max. J. Mack, Cincinnati.
11 J. Burton Parsons, Cleveland,
12 Wm. P. Wiltsee, Cincinnati,
13 Stith M. Sullivan, Dayton,
14 Benjamin F. Rees, Columbus,
15 Sheldon Sickles, Cleveland,
16 Charles E. Bliven, Toledo,
17 Charles A. Collins, Akron,
18 Gabriel B. Harman, Dayton,
19 W. L. Buechner, Youngstown,
20 Theodore B. Gordon, Columbus,
21 Andrew Nemback, Cincinnati,
22 George R. Sage, Cincinnati,
23 Henry H. Tatem, Cincinnati,
24 E. S. Whitaker, Garretsville,
25 Eli Fasold, Dayton,
26 Henry W. Bigelow, Toledo,
27 George W. Hart, Toledo,
28 John D. Caldwell, Cincinnati,

29 David N. Kiusmau, Columbus,   30 Alex. G. Patton, Columbus,
31 Martin J. Houck, Dayton,   32 John W. Chamberlin, Tiffin,
33 Alex. F. Vance, Jr., Urbana,   34 Robert V. Hampson, Salem,
35 Calvin Halladay, Lima,   36 Joseph KcK. Goodspeed, Athens,
37 William B. Melish, Cincinnati,   38 Sam Briggs, Cleveland,
39 David C. Winegarner, Newark,   40 William Shepard, Columbus,
41 Eben J. Cutler, Cleveland,   42 Edward D. Page, Cleveland,
43 Robert Gwynn, Cincinnati.   44 Frederick W. Pelton, Cleveland,
45 William J. Akers, Cleveland.   46 David L. King, Akron,
47 Huntingtou Brown, Mansfield,   48 Sidney Moore, Delaware,
49 Joseph H. Duun, Columbus,   50 John T. Harris, Columbus,
51 C. W. Chamberlain, Dayton,   52 Edward W. Matthews, Cambridge,
53 Clarence E. Armstrong, Toledo,   54 Barton Smith, Toledo,
55 Joseph A. Stipp, Toledo,   56 Charles H. Flack, Cincinnati,
57 William Michie, Cincinnati,   58 Charles H. Tucker, Cleveland,
59 Charles E. Stanley, Cleveland,   60 Samuel S. Williams, Newark,
61 Otho L. Hayes, Galion,   62 John W. Parsons, Springfield,
63 Allen Jeffers, Dayton,   64 Orestes A. B. Lenter, Columbus,
65 James A. Collins, Cincinnati,   66 Fred A. Morse, Cleveland,
67 LaFayette Lyttle, Toledo,   68 John N. Bell, Dayton,
69 Levi C. Goodale, Cincinnati.

INDIANA.

1 James W. Hess, Indianapolis,   2 George H. Fish, N. Y. City,
3 Nathaniel F. Bonsall, New Albany,   4 Joseph W. Smith, Indianapolis,
5 Henry G. Thayer, Plymouth,   6 Gilbert W. Davis,   "
7 Chas. E. Wright, Indianapolis,   8 Martin H. Rice,   "
9 Sydney W. Douglas, Evansville,   10 Jacob W. Smith,   "
11 Walter Vail, Michigau City,   12 John L. Butler, Vincennes,
13 William J. Robie, Richmond,   14 Austin H. Brown, Indianapolis,
15 Byion K. Elliott, Indianapolis.   16 John T. Brush,   "
17 Henry C. Adams,   "   18 Bruce Carr,   "
19 Thos. S. McKiuley, Crawfordsv.,   20 Samuel B. Sweet, Fort Wayne,
21 Samuel A. Wilson, Muncie.   22 William Hacker, Shelbyville,
23 Wm. H. Smythe, Indianapolis,   24 Cyrill B. Cole, Seymour,
25 John W. Craft, Terre Haute,   26 Robert Van Valsah, Terre Haute,
27 Joseph L. Smith, Richmond,   28 James B. Safford, Columbus,
29 Roscoe O. Hawkins, Indianapolis,   30 Mortimer Nye, La Porte,
31 Thomas R. Long, Terre Haute,   32 Henry A. Moyer, Kendallville,
33 Jos. A. Manning, Michigan City,   34 George W. Pixley, Fort Wayue,
35 William Geake, Fort Wayne,   36 Geo. E. Farrington, Terre Haute,
37 Jacob D. Leighty, St. Joe.

ILLINOIS.

1 William H. Turner, Chicago,   2 Henry C. Ranuey, Chicago,
3 Enoch B. Stevens,   "   4 William H. Gale,   "
5 Benjamin F. Patrick, "   6 James H. Field,   "
7 Alden C. Millard,   "   8 Loyal L. Munn, Freeport,

9 Eugene B. Myers, Chicago,
10 Wiley M. Eagan, Chicago,
11 Horatius N. Hurlburt, "
12 Jacob W. Brewer, Monmouth,
13 Warner G. Purdy, "
14 Fred A. Wheeler, Baltimore, Md.,
15 Henry H. Getty, "
16 James H. McVicker, Chicago,
17 Henry H. Pond, "
18 Gilbert W. Barnard, "
19 De Witt C. Creiger, "
20 James A. Hawley, Dixon,
21 Jacob W. Skinkle, "
22 John O'Neil, Chicago,
23 Jonathan A. Allen, "
24 James B. Bradwell, "
25 Haswell C. Clark, Kankakee,
26 John McLaren, "
27 Amos Pettibone, Chicago,
28 Alfred Russell, "
29 Edgar P. Tobey "
30 James E. Church, "
31 James Bannister, Peoria,
32 Geo. R. McClellan, "
33 Robert M. Johnson, Chicago,
34 William E. Poulson, "
35 Edward C. Page, Ashley,
36 John M. Pearson, Godfrey,
37 Charles F. Hitchcock, Peoria,
38 De Laskie Miller, Chicago,
39 Lloyd D. Richardson, Chicago,
40 John P. Nowell, Danville,
41 Wm. Lee Roy Milligan, Ottaway,
42 George M. Moulton, Chicago,
43 Eliakim R. Bliss, Chicago,
44 Isaac C. Edwards, Peoria,
45 George W. Warvelle "
46 Charles K. Herrick, Chicago,
47 Charles F. Gunther, "
48 Edward S. Mulliner, Quincy,
49 Joseph M. Bailey, Freeport,
50 Michael Stoskopf, Freeport,
51 Eug. Le Compte Stocker, Cent'a,
52 Joseph Spies, Chicago,
53 Norman T. Gassette, Chicago,
54 George W. Curtis, Peoria.

MICHIGAN.

1 John D. Jennings, Grand Rapids,
2 William Corbin, Adrian,
3 William P. Innes, "
4 Charles H. Brown, Grand Rapids,
5 Charles H. Putnam, Hudson,
6 James Trenton, Detroit,
7 Augustus B. Taber, Detroit,
8 Andrew J. Kellogg, "
9 Richard A. Bury, Adrian,
10 Charles T. Hills, Muskegon,
11 Osias W. Shipman, Detroit,
12 Perrin V. Fox, Grand Rapids,
13 Benjamin F. Haxton, "
14 Henry F. Hastings, "
15 Darius D. Thorp, "
16 William H. Baxter, Detroit,
17 Daniel Striker, Hastings,
18 Frank Henderson, Kalamazoo,
19 Charles M. Wheeler, Marquette,
20 Charles H. Pomeroy, Bay City,
21 Richard D. Swartout, Gr. Rapids,
22 John B. Corliss, Detroit,
23 Nicholas Coulson, Detroit,
24 M. Howard Chamberlain, Detroit,
25 Frank O. Gilbert, Bay City,
26 Francis M. Moore, Marquette,
27 Edgar M. Sharp, "
28 Wm. C. Maybury, Detroit,
29 Joseph H. Steele, Sault Ste Marie.

WISCONSIN.

1 Melvin L. Youngs, Milwaukee,
2 William T. Palmer, Milwaukee,
3 Samuel F. Greely, Chicago, Ill.,
4 Jared W. Crippen, "
5 Wm. T. Galloway, Eau Claire,
6 Francis M. Wilkinson, "
7 Michael J. Haisler, Milwaukee,
8 Fred L. Von Suessmilch, Delevan,
9 Charles D. Rogers, "
10 Henry S. Bracken, Milwaukee,
11 Geo. H. Beezenberg, "
12 Wm. H. Brazier, "

13 Oliver Libbey, Green Bay,　　14 Francis J. Crosby, Milwaukee,
15 Jerome A. Watrous, Milwaukee, 16 Sidney H. Cole,　　"
17 Edward J. Stark,　　　"　　18 Elias G. Jackson, Oshkosh,
19 Nathan B. Rundle, Eau Claire, 20 Samuel S. Fifield, Ashland,
21 Homer S. Goss, Portage,　　22 Joel W. Bingham, Milwaukee.
　　　23 Matthias R. Teegarden, Racine City.

Non-Resident Honorary Members.

1 James C. L. Wadsworth.............. ....San Francisco, Cal.
2 William Filmer,...　　"　　"
3 Harmon G. Reynolds...Blue Rapids, Kansas

Subordinate Bodies.

Consistories S. P. R. S. 32°.

1 MAINE...Portland, Maine
2 EDWARD A. RAYMOND.......................... ....Nashua, New Hampshire
3 VERMONT..Burlington, Vermont
4 MASSACHUSETTS...Boston, Massachusetts
5 RHODE ISLAND..Providence, Rhode Island
6 LAFAYETTE..Bridgeport, Connecticut
7 CONNECTICUT SOVEREIGN.................................Norwich,　　"
8 ALBANY...Albany, New York
9 NEW YORK CITY...New York City,　　"
10 CENTRAL...Syracuse,　　"
11 OTSENINGO...Binghampton,　　"
12 ROCHESTER...Rochester,　　"
13 CORNING...Corning,　　"
14 AURORA GRATA...Brooklyn,　　"
15 NEW JERSEY..................................... ....Jersey City, New Jersey
16 EXCELSIOR...Camden,　　"
17 PENNSYLVANIA..Pittsburgh, Pennsylvania
18 PHILADELPHIA..Philadelphia,　　"
19 HARRISBURG..Harrisburg,　　"
20 CALDWELL...Bloomsburg,　　"
21 KEYSTONE...Scranton,　　"
22 MICHIGAN...Detroit, Michigan
23 DE WITT CLINTON...Grand Rapids,　　"
24 OHIO...Cincinnati, Ohio
25 NORTHERN OHIO...Cleveland,　　"
26 INDIANA....... ....Indianapolis, Indiana
27 ORIENTAL..Chicago, Illinois
28 QUINCY...Quincy,　　"
29 FREEPORT..Freeport,　　"
30 PEORIA..Peoria,　　"
31 WISCONSIN..Milwaukee, Wisconsin

Total No. of Members of 32°, 12,850.　Average, 414½.

Chapters of Rose Croix, 18°.

1	DUNLAP	Portland, Maine
2	BANGOR	Bangor, Maine
3	ST. GEORGE	Nashua, New Hampshire
4	NEW HAMPSHIRE	Portsmouth, "
5	DELTA	Burlington, Vermont
6	MOUNT CALVARY	Lowell, Massachusetts
7	MOUNT OLIVET	Boston, "
8	LAWRENCE	Worcester, "
9	RHODE ISLAND	Providence, Rhode Island
10	PEQUONNOCK	Bridgeport, Connecticut
11	NORWICH	Norwich, "
12	NEW HAVEN	New Haven, "
13	ALBANY	Albany, New York
14	NEW YORK CITY	New York City, "
15	CENTRAL CITY	Syracuse, "
16	AURORA GRATA	Brooklyn, "
17	OTSENINGO	Binghampton, "
18	ROCHESTER	Rochester, "
19	CORNING	Corning, "
20	DELTA	Troy, "
21	YAH-NUN-DAH-SIS	Utica, "
22	TRENTON	Trenton, New Jersey
23	JERSEY CITY	Jersey City, "
24	EXCELSIOR	Camden, "
25	ADONIRAM	Paterson, "
26	OLIVET	New Brunswick, "
27	PITTSBURGH	Pittsburgh, Pennsylvania
28	KILWINNING	Philadelphia
29	HARRISBURG	Harrisburg, "
30	EVERGREEN	Bloomsburg, Pennsylvania
31	KEYSTONE	Scranton, "
32	MOUNT OLIVET	Detroit, Michigan
33	ROBINSON	Grand Rapids, "
34	SAGINAW VALLEY	Bay City, "
35	PENINSULA	Marquette, "
36	CINCINNATI	Cincinnati, Ohio
37	ARIEL	Cleveland, "
38	COLUMBUS	Columbus, "
39	DAYTON	Dayton, "
40	CAMBRIDGE	Cambridge, "
41	FORT INDUSTRY	Toledo, "
42	INDIANAPOLIS	Indianapolis, Indiana
43	PEORIA	Peoria, Illinois
44	GOURGAS	Chicago, "
45	QUINCY	Quincy, "
46	FREEPORT	Freeport, "
47	WISCONSIN	Milwaukee, Wisconsin

Total No. of Members 12,764, Average 271½.

Councils of Princes of Jerusalem, 16°.

1	PORTLAND	Portland, Maine
2	AUBURN	Auburn, "
3	PALESTINE	Bangor, "
4	GRAND COUNCIL	Portsmouth, New Hampshire
5	ORIENTAL	Nashua, " "
6	JOSEPH W. ROBY	Burlington, Vermont
7	MOUNT CALVARY	Montpelier, "
8	LOWELL	Lowell, Massachusetts
9	GILES F. YATES	Boston, "
10	MASSASOIT	Springfield, "
11	GODDARD	Worcester, "
12	RHODE ISLAND	Providence, Rhode Island
13	WASHINGTON	Bridgeport, Connecticut
14	VAN RENSSELAER	Norwich, "
15	ELM CITY	New Haven, "
16	HARTFORD	Hartford, "
17	GRAND COUNCIL	Albany, New York
18	NEW YORK CITY	New York City, "
19	CENTRAL	Syracuse, "
20	AURORA GRATA	Brooklyn, "
21	OTSENINGO	Binghampton, "
22	ROCHESTER	Rochester, "
23	CORNING	Corning, "
24	PALMONI	Buffalo, "
25	DELTA	Troy, "
26	YAH-NUN-DAH-SIS	Utica, "
27	MERCER	Trenton, New Jersey
28	EXCELSIOR	Camden, "
29	JERSEY CITY	Jersey City, "
30	ADONIRAM	Patterson, "
31	ZERUBBABEL	New Brunswick, "
32	PENNSYLVANIA	Pittsburg, Pennsylvania
33	DE JOINVILLE	Philadelphia, "
34	HARRISBURG	Harrisburg, "
35	ZERUBBABEL	Bloomsburg, "
36	KEYSTONE	Scranton, "
37	CARSON	Detroit, Michigan
38	CYRUS	Grand Rapids, "
39	BAY CITY	Bay City, "
40	LAKE SUPERIOR	Marquette, "
41	DALCHO	Cincinnati, Ohio
42	CAMBRIDGE	Cambridge, "
43	BAHURIM	Cleveland, "
44	FRANKLIN	Columbus, "
45	MIAMI	Dayton, "
46	NORTHERN LIGHT	Toledo, "

```
47  SERAIAH.....................................................Indianapolis, Indiana
48  DARIUS...........................................................Fort Wayne,        "
49  CHICAGO.........................................................Chicago, Illinois
50  PEORIA.............................................................Peoria,        "
51  QUINCY............................................................Quincy,        "
52  FREEPORT..........................................................Freeport,      "
53  WISCONSIN......................................................Milwaukee, Wisconsin
```

Total No. of Members 16°, 13,290, Average, 250⅔.

Lodges of Perfection, 14°.

```
 1  YATES..............................................................Portland, Maine
 2  LEWISTON.........................................................Lewiston,        "
 3  EASTERN STAR .................................................Bangor,          "
 4  INEFFABLE.................... .... Portsmouth, New Hampshire
 5  AARON P. HUGHES.....................................Nashua,        "        "
 6  HASWELL.........................................................Burlington, Vermont
 7  WINDSOR........................................................Windsor,         "
 8  GAMALIEL WASHBURNE.............................Montpelier,      "
 9  BENNINGTON...............................................Bennington,       "
10  MIZPAH.........................................................St. Johnsbury,    "
11  BOSTON........................................................Boston, Massachusetts
12  LOWELL.........................................................Lowell,          "
13  LAFAYETTE ..................................................Boston,           "
14  WORCESTER...................................................Worcester,        "
15  SUTTON.........................................................Salem,           "
16  EVENING STAR...............................................Springfield,       "
17  SOLOMON'S..................................................Providence, Rhode Island
18  VAN RENSSELAER.........................................Newport,          "
19  DE WITT CLINTON.....................................Bridgeport, Connecticut
20  KING SOLOMON............................................Norwich,          "
21  CHARTER OAK...............................................Hartford,         "
22  E. G. STORER...............................................New Haven,        "
23  INEFFABLE....................................................Albany, New York
24  NEW YORK CITY.........................................New York City, New York
25  CENTRAL CITY..............................................Syracuse,        "
26  AURORA GRATA ...........................................Brooklyn,        "
27  OTSENINGO..................................................Binghampton,     "
28  ROCHESTER..................................................Rochester,       "
29  CORNING.....................................................Corning,         "
30  PALMONI,....................................................Buffalo,         "
31  DELTA.........................................................Troy,           "
32  YAH-NUN-DAH-SIS.......................................Utica,          "
33  GERMANIA........................................... ........Rochester,       "
34  LOCK CITY..................................................Lockport,        "
35  WATERTOWN...............................................Watertown,       "
36  ST. LAWRENCE ...........................................Potsdam,         "
37  NORTHERN STAR..........................................Plattsburgh,     "
```

38	MERCER	Trenton, New Jersey
39	JERSEY CITY	Jersey City, "
40	EXCELSIOR	Camden, "
41	NEW BRUNSWICK	New Brunswick, "
42	ADONIRAM	Paterson, "
43	GOURGAS	Pittsburg, Pennsylvania
44	PHILADELPHIA	Philadelphia, "
45	HARRISBURG	Harrisburg, "
46	ENOCH	Bloomsburg, "
47	LANCASTER	Lancaster, "
48	KEYSTONE	Scranton, "
49	PRESQUE ISLE	Erie, "
50	TOWANDA	Towanda, "
51	CARSON	Detroit, Michigan
52	MORIAH	Grand Rapids, "
53	DETROIT	Detroit, "
54	McCORMICK	Bay City, "
55	MARQUETTE	Marquette, "
56	GIBULUM	Cincinnati, Ohio
57	CAMBRIDGE	Cambridge, "
58	ELIADAH	Cleveland, "
59	ENOCH	Columbus, "
60	GABRIEL	Dayton, "
61	MI-A-MI	Toledo, "
62	ADONIRAM	Indianapolis, Indiana
63	FORT WAYNE	Fort Wayne, "
64	VAN RENSSELAER	Chicago, Illinois
65	QUINCY	Quincy, "
66	FREEPORT	Freeport, "
67	CENTRAL CITY	Peoria, "
68	WISCONSIN	Milwaukee, Wisconsin

Total number of members of 14°, 15,378, Average, 226 1-7.

GRAND BODIES

OF THE

Ancient and Accepted Scottish Rite,

RECOGNIZED BY AND

In Relations of Amity with the Supreme Councils, 33°,
for the Southern and Northern Jurisdictions
of the United States of America,

AND THE

M. W. Grand Lodge of Free and Accepted Masons of the State of California.

Supreme Council, 33°, for France and Dependencies

LOUIS PROAL, Paris,...............................*M. P. Sov. Gr. Commander*
EMMANUEL ARAGO, Paris,..........................*Lieut. Grand Commander*
JEAN BAPTISTE BAGARY,..........................*Secretary General, H. E.*
EUGENE BERARD,........................*Grand Chancellor and K. of the Seals*

GRAND REPRESENTATIVES OF AND TO THE SUPREME COUNCILS OF THE
SOUTHERN AND NORTHERN JURISDICTIONS OF THE UNITED
STATES OF AMERICA, RESPECTIVELY.

EUGENE BERARD, (S)
MAURICE SCHWALB, (N)
ACHILLE REGULUS MOREL, (S) ....Oakland, California
ANTHONY EUGENE STOCKER, (N) ....Philadelphia, Penn.
Address of the Secretariat, Grand Chancellor and
Secretary General,..........................42 Rue Rochechouart, Paris

---

Supreme Council, 33°, for England, Wales and Dependencies of the British Crown.

H. R. H. ALBERT EDWARD, PRINCE OF WALES, K. G. 33° GRAND PATRON
THE EARL OF LATHAM,..........................*M. P. Sov. Grand Commander*
CAPT. NATHANIEL GEORGE PHILLIPS,............*Lieut. Grand Commander*
LIEUT. COL. SHADWELL H. CLERKE,...............*Grand Secretary General*
HUGH DAVID SANDEMAN,.....*Grand Secretary of Foreign Correspondence*

GRAND REPRESENTATIVES OF AND TO THE SUPREME COUNCILS, 33° FOR
THE SOUTHERN AND NORTHERN JURISDICTIONS OF THE
UNITED STATES OF AMERICA.

CAPT. NATHANIEL GEORGE PHILLIPS, (S. and N.) 33° Golden Square
London.

THEODORE SUTTON PARVIN, (S) ....Iowa City, Iowa
CLINTON FREEMAN PAIGE, (N) ....Binghampton, New York
Address of the Secretariat, ...33 Golden Square, London

Supreme Council, 33°, for Scotland.

FRANCIS ROBERT ST. CLAIR ERSKINE, Earl of Rosslyn,
M. P. Sov. Grand Commander
EARL OF MAR AND KELLIE,...........................*Lieut. Grand Commander*
LINDSAY MACKERSY............................*Grand Secretary General, H. E.*

GRAND REPRESENTATIVES OF AND TO THE SUPREME COUNCILS OF THE
SOUTHERN AND NORTHERN JURISDICTIONS OF THE
UNITED STATES OF AMERICA.

EARL OF KINTORE, (S)
FRANCIS ROBERT ST. CLAIR ERSKINE, EARL OF ROSSLYN, (N) Edinburg
NATHANIEL LEVIN, (S) ....Charleston, South Carolina
CHARLES LEVI WOODBURY, (N)..Boston, Mass.
Address of the Secretariat, ...No. 3 St. David Street, Edinburg

Supreme Council, 33°, for Ireland.

JOHN FITZHENRY TOWNSEND..................*M. P. Sov. Grand Commander*
RIGHT HON. HEDGES EYRE CHATTERTON......*Lieut. Grand Commander*
E. W. MAUNSELLI...............................*Grand Secretary General, H. E.*

GRAND REPRESENTATIVES OF AND TO THE SUPREME COUNCILS FOR
THE SOUTHERN AND NORTHERN JURISDICTIONS OF THE
UNITED STATES OF AMERICA.

JOHN FITZHENRY TOWNSEND (S)...Dublin
E. W. MAUNSELLI (N)...................................... .... "
FREDERICK WEBBER (S)................. ....Louisville, Kentucky
BENJAMIN DEAN (N)............. ....Boston, Mass.
Address of the Secretariat, No. 30 Upper Fitzwillian Street, Dublin.

Supreme Council, 33°, for Belgium.

PIERRE VAN HUMBECK...........................*M. P. Sov. Grand Commander*
DR. JEAN CROCQ...*Lieut. Grand Commander*
GUSTAV WASHER.............*Grand Chancellor, Secretary General. H. E.*

GRAND REPRESENTATIVES OF AND TO THE SUPREME COUNCILS FOR
THE SOUTHERN AND NORTHERN JURISDICTIONS OF THE
UNITED STATES OF AMERICA.

GUSTAV WASHER, (S and N.)
Address of the Secretariat, ...114 Avenue Louise, Bruxelles

REPRESENTATIVES OF AND TO THE M. W. GRAND LODGE OF F. & A. M.
OF THE STATE OF CALIFORNIA.

GUSTAVE JOTTRAND...Brussels
ALEXANDER G. ABELL............................San Francisco, California

Supreme Council, 33°, for Spain.

MANUEL LLANO Y PERSE,................ ....*M. P. Sov. Grand Commander*
JUAN UTOR Y FERNANDEZ,..................*Grand Secretary General, H. E.*

GRAND REPRESENTATIVES OF AND TO THE SUPREME COUNCILS OF THE
SOUTHERN AND NORTHERN JURISDICTIONS OF THE
UNITED STATES OF AMERICA.

JUAN UTOR Y FERNANDEZ,
....(S) Vacant.
ENOCH T. CARSON, (N) ....Cincinnati, Ohio

GRAND REPRESENTATIVES OF AND TO THE M. W. GRAND LODGE OF
F. & A. M., OF THE STATE OF CALIFORNIA.

JULIO FERNANDEZ ESPINA, ...Madrid
ALEXANDER G. ABELL, ...San Francisco, Cal.

Grande Orient Lusitano Unido Supremo Conselho, 33°, de Maconaria Portugueja.

AUGOSTO SEBASTIAO DE CASTRO GUEDES, *M. P. Sov. Grand Commander*
GENERAL VICONDE DE FARO,......................*Lieut. Grand Commander*
EDUARDO AMOROUS,..........................*Grand Secretary General, H. E.*

GRAND REPRESENTATIVES OF AND TO THE SUPREME COUNCILS, 33° FOR
THE SOUTHERN AND NORTHERN JURISDICTIONS OF
THE UNITED STATES OF AMERICA.

REV. THOMAS GODFREY P. POPE, (S) ....Rue de Estreila 4, Lisbon
DR. ANTONIO M. DA CUNHA BELLEM, (N) ....Lisbon
....(S) Vacant.
....(N) Vacant.

GRAND REPRESENTATIVES OF AND TO THE M. W. GRAND LODGE OF
F. & A. M., OF THE STATE OF CALIFORNIA.

LUIZ FILLIPPE DA MATTA,............... ....Lisbon
WILLIAM CALDWELL BELCHER, P. G. M.,......................Marysville, Cal.

Unico Supreme Consiglio Del 33°, per L'Italia.
SEDENTE IN ROME.

DR. TIMOTEO RIBOLI, } *Grand Commanders, Hon. ad vitem.*
GIORGIO TAMJO.
ADRIANO LEMMI,...*M. P. Grand Commander*

COL. GIOVANNI CECCONI,.............................*Lieut. Grand Commander*
PROF. GIOVANNI BOBIO,.............................*Grand Minister of State*
TEOFILO GAY,.............................*Grand Secretary Chancellor*
CESARE COREA,............................. ....*Grand Treasurer Almoner*
LUIGI ORLANDO,.............................*Grand Keeper of Seals*
MARCHESE BENJAMINO PANDOLFI,....................*Grand Standard Bearer*
ALESSANDRO PALUMBO,.............................*Grand Master of Ceremonies*
COL. EDOARDO DE BARTOLOMEIS,...............*Grand Captain of the Guards*

REPRESENTATIVES OF AND TO THE SUPREME COUNCILS FOR THE NORTH-
ERN AND SOUTHERN JURISDICTIONS OF THE UNITED
STATES OF AMERICA.

TIMOTEO RIBOLI, (S) ....29 via: Accademia Albertina, Torino, Italia
TEOFILO GAY, ...Rome
ODELL SQUIRE LONG,(S) ....Wheeling, West Virginia
SAMUEL C. LAWRENCE, (N) ....Boston, Mass.
  Address of the Grand Commander,................................Rome

---

Valley of the Sebeto.

SECTION OF THE SUPREME COUNCIL OF ITALY, FOR THE NEAPOLITAN
PROVINCE.

PROF. MICHELE REUTA,...................................*President of the Section*
ALESSANDRO PALUMBO,.................... ....*Lieut. Grand Commander*
COSMA PANUNZI,...*Grand Secretary Chancellor*
  Address of the Grand Secretary, ...17 Mergellina, Napoli, Italia

---

Valley of the Arno.

SECTION OF THE SUPREME COUNCIL OF ITALY, FOR THE VALLEY OF
THE ARNO. SEE AT LIVORNO.

ANSELMO CARPI,...*President of the Section*
EDOARDO DE BARTOLOMEIS,........................... ....*Vice-President*
FORTUNATO LABI,...*Grand Secretary*

Supreme Council, 88°, pour la Suisse.

SEE AT LAUSANNE.

LOUIS RUCHONNET,...................................*M. P. Sov. Grand Commander*
JULES DALACRETAZ,...............................*Grand Secretary General, H. E.*

GRAND REPRESENTATIVES OF AND TO THE SUPREME COUNCILS FOR
THE SOUTHERN AND NORTHERN JURISDICTIONS OF
THE UNITED STATES OF AMERICA.

EUGENE DU LON, (S)...Vevay
REV. TH. REDARD, (N)......................,.........................Lausanne
WILLIAM OSCAR ROOME, (S) ....Washington, D. C.
HOSMER A. JOHNSON, (N) ....:..........................Chicago, Illinois
  Address of the Grand Secretariat, ...Place du Tunnel, 9 Lausanne

Magyarország, Os Gs Glf. Sk. Sz., 33°, As Nagy Tanacsnak.

Supreme Council, 33°, of Hungary.

SEE AT BUDAPEST.

GEORGE JOANNOVIES, (JOANNOVIES GYORGY) Member of Parliament
and of the Academy of Sciences,........*M. P. Sov. Grand Commander*
ANTOINE SCHNEIDER, (SCHNEIDER ANTAL).................*Grand Chancellor*

GRAND REPRESENTATIVES OF AND TO THE SUPREME COUNCILS, 33°, FOR
THE SOUTHERN AND NORTHERN JURISDICTIONS OF THE
UNITED STATES OF AMERICA.

JULES ZADOR, (ZADOR GUYULA) (S) *Counsellor in the Royal
Ministry of Justice*.....................................Vaczi ut 6, Budapest
.....................................(N) Vacant.
JOHN COMMINGERS AINSWORTH, (S) ....Oakland, California
.....................................(N) Vacant.
Address of the Grand Secretariat, ...Vaczi Boulevard, 45 Budapest

---

Τὸ ΥΠΑΤΟΝ "ΕΑΛΗΝΙΚΟΝ 'ΣΥΜΒΟΥΛΙΟΝ" τοῦ Βαθμοῦ".

Supreme Council, 33°, of Greece.

SEE AT ATHENS.

PRINCE DEMETRIUS RHODSCANAKIS,.........*M. P. Sov. Grand Commander*
NIKOLAOS DAMASKINOS,............................*P. Lieut. Grand Commander*
ANDREAS KALYVAS,...............................*Grand Secretary General, H. E.*

GRAND REPRESENTATIVES OF AND TO THE SUPREME COUNCILS, 33° FOR
THE SOUTHERN AND NORTHERN JURISDICTIONS OF
THE UNITED STATES OF AMERICA.

NIKOLAOS DAMASKINOS, (S).....................................Athens
ANDREAS KALYVAS, (N).....................................Athens
.....................................(S) Vacant.
GEORGE W. DEERING, (N).....................................Portland, Maine

---

Supreme Council, 33°, for Egypt.

SEE AT CAIRO.

S. A. ZOLA.................................*M. Sov. Grand Commander*
FRANCESCO FERDINANDO ODDI,...........*Grand Secretary General, H. E.*

GRAND REPRESENTATIVES OF AND TO THE SUPREME COUNCILS, 33° FOR
THE SOUTHERN AND NORTHERN JURISDICTIONS OF
THE UNITED STATES OF AMERICA.

DOCTOR ABBATE BEY, (S).....................................Cairo
S. A. ZOLA, (N).....................................Cairo
CLEMENT WELLS BENNETT, (S) ....Washington, D. C.
DANIEL SICKELS, (N) ....New York City, N. Y.

GRAND REPRESENTATIVES OF AND TO THE M. W. GRAND LODGE OF
F. & A. M., OF THE STATE OF CALIFORNIA.

FRANCISCO F. ODDI,...Alexandria
ALEX. G. ABELL, (G. S.)...................................San Francisco, Cal.

Supreme Council, 88°, for Tunis.

SEE AT TUNIS.

GUSTAV DESMONS, ...*M. P. Sov. Grand Commander*
NICOLO S. CASSANELLO......................*Grand Secretary General, H. E.*

GRAND REPRESENTATIVES OF AND TO THE SUPREME COUNCILS, 33°, FOR
THE SOUTHERN AND NORTHERN JURISDICTIONS OF
THE UNITED STATES OF AMERICA.

COSIMO S. BURLIZZI, (N)..Tunis.
NICOLO S. CASSANELLO, (N)..Tunis
WILLIAM M. IRELAND, (S).............. ....Washington, D. C.

Supreme Council, 88°, for the Dominion of Canada.

SEE AT MONTREAL.

JOHN VALENTINE ELLIS, St. John. N. B., *M. P. Sov. Grand Commander*
JOHN WALTER MURTON, ...*Lieut. Grand Commander*
HUGH MURRAY, Hamilton, Ontario,........*Grand Secretary General, H. E.*

REPRESENTATIVES OF AND TO THE SUPREME COUNCILS, FOR THE SOUTH-
ERN AND NORTHERN JURISDICTIONS OF THE
UNITED STATES OF AMERICA.

JOHN WALTER MURTON, (S)............................Hamilton, Ontario
HUGH A. MACKAY, (N)...................................... "   "
FREDERICK WEBBER, (S)...............................Louisville, Kentucky
D. BURNHAM TRACY, (N)..................................Detroit, Michigan

---

Supreme Council, 88°, for Mexico.

SEE AT THE CITY OF MEXICO.

IGNACIO POMBO, ...*M. P. Sov. Grand Commander*
MARIANO ESCOBEDO,.................................*Lieut. Grand Commander*
EUGENIO CHAVERS,.............................*Grand Secretary General, H. E.*

GRAND REPRESENTATIVES OF AND TO THE SUPREME COUNCILS, OF THE
SOUTHERN AND NORTHERN JURISDICTIONS OF
THE UNITED STATES OF AMERICA.

IGNACIO POMBO, (S).............Calle de San Felipe Neri 7, City of Mexico
IGNACIO MARISCAL, (N) .... "   "
PHILLIP C. TUCKER, (S)...................................Galveston, Texas
....(N) Vacant.
    Address of the Grand Secretariat,
                    Calle de Marique, No. 5, City of Mexico.

NOTE—The Supreme Council, 33°, for Mexico, relinquished the control of the Symbolic Degrees when the Grand Lodge for the Federal District of Mexico was constituted, and the Supreme Council, 33° for the Southern Jurisdiction of the United States appointed DON CARLOS PACHECO as its Grand Representative to that body, which in turn appointed WILLIAM REYNOLDS SINGLETON of Washington City, D. C., as its Grand Representative to the Supreme Council, 33°, for the Southern Jurisdiction of the United States.

Supreme Council of Colon, 33°, for Cuba and the West Indies.

SEE AT HAVANA.

JUAN IGNACIO ZUAZO, Marquis de Almeras, *M. P. Sov. Grand Commander*
BENITO J. RIERA..............................*Lieut. Grand Commander*
MANUEL N. OCEJO..............................*Grand Secretary General, H. E.*

GRAND REPRESENTATIVES OF AND TO THE SUPREME COUNCILS, 33°,
FOR THE SOUTHERN AND NORTHERN JURISDICTIONS OF
THE UNITED STATES OF AMERICA.

MANUEL OCEJO, (S)......Apartado de Correos 509, l'Habana, Isla de Cuba
..............................(N) Vacant.
ALBERT PIKE, Gr. Com. (S)..............................Washington, D. C.
ALBERT P. MORIARTY, (N)..........104 Stewart Building, N Y. City, N. Y.
Address of Grand Secretariat, Calle de l'Habana 55, Habana de Cuba

Supreme Council, 33°, for Central America.

SEE AT SAN JOSE, COSTA RICA.

GUILLERMO NANNE,..............................*M. P. Sov. Grand Commander*
FELIX MATOS,..............................*Grand Secretary General, H. E.*

GRAND REPRESENTATIVES TO AND FROM THE SUPREME COUNCILS, 33°,
FOR THE SOUTHERN AND NORTHERN JURISDICTIONS OF THE
UNITED STATES OF AMERICA.

ALOYS K. OSBORNE, (S)..............................San Jose, Costa Rica
LORENZO MONTUFAR, (N)..............................Guatemala
EDWIN BALDRIDGE MACGROTTY, (S)..............................Washington, D. C.
THOMAS R. LUMBARD, (N)..........160 Broadway, New York City, N. Y.
Address of the Grand Secretariat, ...San Jose, Costa Rica

Supreme Council, 33°, for New Grenada.

(NOW UNITED STATES OF COLOMBIA.)
SEE AT CARTAJENA.

JUAN MANUEL GRAU,..............................*M. P. Sov. Grand Commander*
BENJAMIN BAENA,..............................*Lieut. Grand Commander*
CARLOS MERLANO,..............................*Grand Secretary General, H. E.*

GRAND REPRESENTATIVES TO AND FROM THE SUPREME COUNCILS, 33°,
FOR THE SOUTHERN AND NORTHERN JURISDICTIONS OF THE
UNITED STATES OF AMERICA.

..............................(S) Vacant.
RAFAEL HERNANDEZ, (N)..............................Cartajena
..............................(S) Vacant.
CLINTON F. PAIGE, (N)..............................Binghampton, New York

Supreme Council, 33°, for United States of Venezuela

SEE AT CARACAS.

GENERAL JOAQUIN CRESPO,..............................*M. P. Sov. Grand Commander*
DR. VICENTE AMENUAL,..............................*Lieut. Grand Commander*
JESUS MARIA MEDINA,..............................*Grand Secretary General, H. E.*
RAIMUNDO I. ANDUEZA,..............................*Grand Secretary*

GRAND REPRESENTATIVES TO AND FROM THE SUPREME COUNCILS, 33°,
FOR THE SOUTHERN AND NORTHERN JURISDICTIONS OF THE
UNITED STATES OF AMERICA.
EUGENE H. PLUMACHER, 33°, (S), U. S. Cousul General........Maracaibo
....(N) Vacant.
....(S) Vacaut.
....(N) Vacaut.

Supreme Council, 33°, for Brazil.
VALLEY OF LAVRADIO. (SEE AT RIO JANEIRO.)

LUIZ ANTONIO VIEIRA DA SILVA,...........*M. P. Sov. Grand Commander*
O BARAO DE JACEGUAY,................... ....*Lieut. Commander*
JOSE DINIZ VILLASBOAS,.....................*Grand Secretary General, H. E.*
GUSTAVO BRAGA,................................*Secretary General Adjunct*

GRAND REPRESENTATIVES TO AND FROM THE SUPREME COUNCILS, 33°,
FOR THE SOUTHERN AND NORTHERN JURISDICTIONS OF THE
UNITED STATES OF AMERICA.
....(S) Vacant.
DR FRANCISCO JOSE CARDOZA, JR. (N)......................Rio Janeiro
JOHN QUINCY ADAMS FELLOWS, (S)................................New Orleans
HEMAN ELY, (N)..Elyria, Ohio

GRAND REPRESENTATIVES TO AND FROM THE M. W. GRAND LODGE
OF F. & A. M., OF THE STATE OF CALIFORNIA.
RODRIGO A. MACHADA REIS,............... ....Rio de Janeiro
ALEXANDER G. ABELL, 33°, G. S...................................San Francisco

---

Supreme Council, 33°. for Uruguay.
SEE AT MONTEVIDEO.

DR CARLOS DE CASTRO,.............................*M. P. Sov. Grand Commander*
MIGUEL FURRIOL,.......................................*Lieut. Grand Commander*
JUAN M. DE LA SIERRA,........................*Grand Secretary General, H. E.*
BELISARIO CONRADO,........................*Grand Secretary General Adjunct*

GRAND REPRESENTATIVES TO AND FROM THE SUPREME COUNCILS, 33°,
FOR THE SOUTHERN AND NORTHERN JURISDICTIONS OF THE
UNITED STATES OF AMERICA.
....(S) Vacant.
JOHN MAC COLL, (N)...Moutevideo
MARTIN COLLINS, (S)................................St. Louis, Missouri
....(N) Vacant.
Address of the Grand Secretariat, 227 Calle Queguay, Montevideo.

Supreme Council, 33°, for the Argentine Republic.
, SEE AT BUENOS AYRES.

DR. JUAN M. LASSEN.............................*M. P. Sov. Grand Commander*
OTTO E. RECKE................................*Grand Secretary General, H. E.*

GRAND REPRESENTATIVES TO AND FROM THE SUPREME COUNCILS, 33°,
FOR THE SOUTHERN AND NORTHERN JURISDICTIONS
OF THE UNITED STATES OF AMERICA.
....(S) Vacaut.
OTTO E. RECKE, (N)..Buenos Ayres
....(S) Vacant.
....(N) Vacant.
Address of the Grand Secretariat, Calle Congallo, 540, Buenos Ayres

REPRESENTATIVES TO AND FROM THE M. W. GRAND LODGE OF F. & A.
M. OF THE STATE OF CALIFORNIA.
ESTEVAN GUABELLO.......................................Buenos Ayres
WILLIAM CALDWELL BELCHER, P. G. M........................Marysville, Cal.

Supreme Council 33°, for Peru.
SEE AT LIMA.

FRANCISCO JAVIER MANATAGUI...............*M. P. Sov. Grand Commander*
JUAN SANCHEZ SILVA....................................*Lieut. Grand Commander*
JUAN MEYANS...............................*Grand Secretary General, H. E.*
GRAND REPRESENTATIVES TO AND FROM THE SUPREME COUNCILS, 33°,
    FOR THE SOUTHERN AND NORTHERN JURISDICTIONS OF
        THE UNITED STATES OF AMERICA.
....(S) Vacant.
RICARDO H. HARTLEY, (N)............................ ....Lima
....(S) Vacant.
....(N) Vacant.
    Address of the Grand Commander, Calle de Milagro, No. 130, Lima

Supreme Council, 33°, for Chili.
SEE AT VALPARAISO.

J. DE MERINO BENVENTE.......................*M.P. Sov. Grand Commander*
H. PLUNKET BONCHIER.......................*Grand Secretary General, H. E.*
GRAND REPRESENTATIVES TO AND FROM THE SUPREME COUNCILS, 33°,
    FOR THE SOUTHERN AND NORTHERN JURISDICTIONS
        OF THE UNITED STATES OF AMERICA.
....(S) Vacant.
GEORGE H. KENDALL, (N).......................................Valparaiso
....(S) Vacant.
CHARLES W. CARTER, (N)...............................Norwich, Conn.

National Grand Lodge of Sweden and Norway.
SEE AT STOCKHOLM.

HIS MAJESTY OSCAR II......................:....................*Grand Master*
A. HJELMSTIERNA...*Grand Secretary*
GRAND REPRESENTATIVES TO AND FROM THE SUPREME COUNCILS, 33°,
    OF THE SOUTHERN JURISDICTION OF THE UNITED
        STATES OF AMERICA.
KAPTIN JACOB TRINDOLF THORSSELL...................................Stockholm
JAMES CUNNINGHAM BATCHELOR.....................New Orleans, Louisiana

National Grand Lodge of Denmark.
SEE AT COPENHAGEN.

....*Grand Master*
....*Grand Secretary*
GRAND REPRESENTATIVE TO AND FROM THE SUPREME COUNCIL, 33° FOR
    THE SOUTHERN JURISDICTION OF THE UNITED •
        STATES OF AMERICA.
....Vacant
JOHN MILLS BROWNE, Surgeon General U. S. Navy....Washington, D. C.

Grand Lodge of the Federal District of Mexico.
(AT THE CITY OF MEXICO.)

JOSE DE LA PAZ ALVAREZ...*Grand Master*
FRANCISCO P. MONTES DE OCA.....................................*Grand Secretary*
GRAND REPRESENTATIVES TO AND FROM THE SUPREME COUNCIL, 33°,
    FOR THE SOUTHERN JURISDICTION OF THE UNITED STATES
        OF AMERICA.
CARLOS PACHECO... ...City of Mexico
WILLIAM REYNOLDS SINGLETON...............................Washington, D. C.

ROLL

OF

OFFICERS AND MEMBERS

OF

The Masonic Veteran Association

OF THE PACIFIC COAST,

FOR ITS TWELFTH YEAR, 1889–90.

Officers.

W. WILLIAM S. MOSES, P. M. 32°,............San Francisco, Cal., *President*
W. THOMAS G .LAMBERT, P. M. K. T.......Monterey, Cal., *1st Vice-Pres.*
W. ORRIN W. HOLLENBECK, P. M. R. A.......Auburn, Cal., *2d Vice-Pres.*
M. W. CHRISTOPHER TAYLOR, 33°, G. M. G. C. K. T.
                                        Vice-President for Oregon
M. W. LOUIS ZEIGLER, 33°, P. G. M. P. G. H. P.,
                        Vice-President for State of Washington
M. W. HARRY R. COMLY, 33°, P. G. M. K. T.......*Vice-Pres. for Montana*
    " LAWRENCE N. GREENLEAF, 33°, P. G. M. K. T.,
                                Vice-Pres. for Colorado
M. W. JAMES LOWE, 32°, P. G. M. E. C. K. T...   "   "   *Utah*
W. ALEX. D. ROCK, P. M. R. A...................   "   "   *Nevada*
W. JOSEPH V. COWAN, P. M...................*Vice-Pres. for New Mexico*
W. ALEX. G. OLIVER, P. M., G. H. P. K. T.   "   "   *Arizona*
W. M. EDWIN A. SHERMAN, 33°,...................Oakland, Cal., *Secretary*
W. WILLIAM S. PHELPS, P. M...............San Francisco, Cal., *Treasurer*
W. CHARLES H. HAILE, 14°, P. M................. Alameda, Cal., *Marshal*
W. OSGOOD C. WHEELER, P. M. K. T............Oakland, Cal., *Chaplain*
*BERNARD F. STROMBERG, 30°...................Oakland, Cal., *Tiler*

Past Presidents.

W. COLUMBUS WATERHOUSE, 33°, P. M. P. E. C. K. T...........S. F., Cal.

SAMUEL SWIFT, K. T...Oakland, "
JAMES M. McDONALD, 32°, P. G. Tr. K. T...............San Francisco, "
M. W. LEONIDAS E. PRATT, 32°, P. G. M. P. G. H. P., K. T.,
    (deceased)...San Francisco, Cal.
W. WASHINGTON AYER, 32°, P. M......................   "   "   "
ROBERT H. LUCAS, R. A...............................   "   "   "
W. JAMES L. COGSWELL, P. M. R. A...................   "   "   "

Corresponding Secretaries.

*W. Frederick Webber, 33°, P. M., Secretary General, S. C. S. J.,
Washington, D. C.
*Edwin B. Spinney, 14°, K. T..Boston, Mass.
*W. William E. Steuart, P. M.........................Baltimore, Maryland
*M. W. James C. Batchelor, 33°, P. G. M., Grand Secretary
of the Grand Lodge of Louisiana, New Orleans, Louisiana

Members.

CALIFORNIA.

*M. W. P. G. M. Jonathan Drake Stevenson, R. A......San Francisco
*   "   "   John Ashby Tutt...Madison
*   "   "   Benj. Daniel Hyam........................Washington, D. C.
*   "   "   Nathaniel Green Curtis, K. T.............Sacramento
*   "   "   Wm. Caldwell Belcher, 32°, K. T...........Marysville
*   "   "   Gilbert Burnett Claiborne, K. T..............Stockton
*   "   "   Wm. Abraham Davies, 33°, P. G. C. K. T...........S. F.
*   "   "   Isaac Lutvene Titus, 33°, P. G. C. K. T., Phoenix, A.
*   "   "   Geo Clement Perkins, P. G. C. K. T...San Francisco
*   "   "   John Mills Browne, 33°, P. G. H. P. K. T., Wash., D. C.
*   "   "   Samuel Crawford Denson.....................Sacramento
*   "   "   Clay Webster Taylor, 32°, K. T...................Shasta
*   "   "   Wiley James Tinnin, P. G. H. P...........San Francisco
*   "   "   Edmund Clement Atkinson, K. T...........Sacramento
*   "   "   Hiram Newton Rucker, K. T...................Stockton
*   "   "   Morris March Estee, K. T...............................Napa
*R. W. D. G. M. William Johnston, Sr. K. T...................Sacramento
*   "   S. G. W. Charles Ray Gritman, K. T...........................Napa
*   "   J. G. W. Henry Sayre Orme, 32°, P. G. C. K. T. ...Los Angeles
*V. W. G. S. Alexander Gurdon Abell, 33°, P. G. C. K. T..........S. F
    "   Nathan Weston Spaulding, 33°, P. G. H. P. K. T.,......Oakland
*R. W. P. D. G. M. Alvah Russell Conklin...................San Francisco
    R. W. P. S. G. W. Theo. Guevara Cockrill, K. T.......   "
    R. W. P. J. G. W. Jacob Hart Neff, 32°, P. G. H. P. G. G. K. T. Colfax
*V. R. Wm. Henry Hill, P. M. K. T., 32°...........................San Rafael
*W. Charles Dana Barrows, G. Orator, K. T.... ....San Francisco
* " George Johnson, P. M. A. G. S. K. T.....................   "
* " James Wright Anderson, G. L. K. T...................   "
* " James Baunty Stevens, Gr. Mar...................................... Napa
* " Wm. Henry Edwards, Gr. Std. Bearer.....................San Francisco
* " Samuel Bond Hinckley, Gr. Sd. Bearer, K. T...............Riverside
*W. Fred. Wm. Lucas, P. M...Santa Cruz
* " Edward Meyers Preston, S. G. D. K. T...................Nevada City
* " Alex. Douglas Laughlin, J. G. D...........................Santa Rosa
* " Charles Mulholland, S. G. Std.............................Independence
* " Addison Morgan, Jr.   "   ....San Diego
* " Jacob Franklin Boller, G. P..... ....Tulare

*W. SAMUEL DAVID MAYER, G. Org., K. T....................San Francisco
* " JAMES OGLESBY, G. TILER, 32°, K. T......................   "
*V. R. P. G. C. ADAM C. BAINE................................Stockton
*W. P. G. MAR. HARVEY MATTHEWS, K. T....................San Francisco
*   "   SWD. B., WM. HENRY HATTON.........................——
*W   "   S. G. D., JOSEPH CLARENCE WARD, K. T..............Visalia
*"   "   J. " " EUGENE J. CREGORY, K. T................Sacramento
*"   "   Std. ROMAYNE WILLIAMS............................Pasadena
*AKERLY, REV. BENJAMIN, P. M. K. T........................Oakland
*ALEXANDER LOUIS L., 32°.................................   "
*ANDERSON, REV. THOS. HART BENTON, P. M. K. T..............   "
ADAMS, FREDERICK, P. M ....San Luis Obispo
ATKINSON, THOMAS T., P. M........................ ....San Francisco
ALLEN, MORTIMER CHERBURY, P. M. P. H. P. K. T.............Shasta
APPLEGATE, GEORGE WASHINGTON, P. M. R. A.............Applegates
BLAKE, CHARLES EDWARD SR., K. T......................San Francisco
*BASTON, JOSEPH GARDINER, 32°, K. T....................   "
BURKETT, ALEXANDER, 32°, P. M. P. H. P. K. T.............Modesto
BRAMAN, JASON JARVIS, 32°.............. ....Healdsburg
BLOOM, HERMAN, R. A...............................San Luis Obispo
BROWN, ROLAND GAIR, 32°, K. T..........................Oakland
*BROWN, CHARLES F., 33° P. M. K. T....................San Francisco
BROWN, FRANK E., 32°, K. T.............................   "
BROMLEY, GEORGE T., P. M. K. T......................   "
BUFFINGTON, JOHN MASON, 33°, K. T.....................Oakland
BADGER, WILLIAM G., K. T.............................Fruitvale
*BISHOP, AMASA WRIGHT, 30°, P. M. K. T.................Oakland
*BUTTON, FRED LAWRENCE, P. M...........................   "
BUSCELLE, JAMES R..................................San Francisco
BELLAMY, BENSON C., P. M. P. H. P.......................Covelo
BOWNE, WILLIAM STEBBINS, 14°, P. M...................Santa Clara
BOOTH, LUCIUS ANSON...............................Oakland
BURNHAM, CHARLES F., 32°, E. C. K. T..................   "
*BELL, REV. SAMUEL BOOKSTIVER.........................   "
BIGELOW, CHARLES EDWIN, R. A........................San Francisco
BYSTLE, DANIEL, P. M. R. A. ....——
*CASWELL, THOMAS HUBBARD, 33°, P. M. P. G. H. P. P. E.
        G. C. G. Chancellor Sup. Con. S. J. U. S.............San Francisco
CLARK, TREAT P., 32°.................................   "
CALDWELL, JOHN C....................................Monterey
COTTRELL, EDWARD MORTIMER, 32°, P. M............San Francisco
CRELLIN, JOHN, K. T..................................Oakland
*CLARK, ALVAH K., P. M. H. P...........................   "
*CRAWFORD, ELLISON L. P. M. H. P........................Georgetown
*CRESSY, EDWARD P.   "   " K. T...................San Francisco
*CROCKER, CHARLES F., 32°, K. T.......................   "
*CAMPBELL, WALTER M., K. T...........................   "

*Campbell, Fred McLean, R. A...Oakland
  Davis, Wm. Wallace, K. T..   "
*Cole, Rector E., P. M. R. A..   "
  Dick, Byron Coleman, 32°..   "
*Dewey, Alfred T......:...   "
  Dorwin, George W...Melrose
*Day, Franklin H., 32°, P. M. G. H. P. P. E. C. K. T......San Francisco
*Dorn, Marcellus A., 32°, P. M. K. T............................   "
*Davis, William B., K. T..Sacramento
*Dusenbury, John B., K. T......... ....   "
  Edgar, Daniel J., 32°...San Francisco
  Evers, John Henry, R. A..Oakland
  Escolle, Honore..Monterey
  Eveland, George F...San Francisco
  Ellis, Joseph Doane...   "
*Ewer, Warren B., K. T..   "
  Figel, Joseph R. A...   "
  Fronk, George...Oakland
  Fuller, Amos Leighton, R. A..   "
  Fisher, George W...   "
*Fisher, Phillip M..   "
  Filmer, William, 33°..San Francisco
  Fletcher, Le Roy Dermott, 18°.....................................San Francisco
  Flint, Thomas Sr., P. M. P. H. P. K. T......................South San Juan
*Fox, Charles N., K. T...Oakland
  Graves, Hiram T., 32°, P. M., P. G. H. P., P. G. C.........San Francisco
  Goad, William Frank, P. M. K. T.................................   "
  Gillett, Charles Edwin, 33°, P. M., P. H. P. P. Th. I. M.
                          P. G. C. K. T.....................................Oakland
  Gibbs, William T., P. M..   "
*Grimes, George L...San Francisco
  Goud, George L., 32°, K. T..   "
  Gilpin, Zachary T., 32°, P. E. C. K. T..........................Oakland
*Gray, Spaulding, K. T..————
  Goodman, George, 32°, R. A..Oakland
  Gardner, James T., K. T...   "
  Gibbons, William P...Alameda
  Holliday, Samuel W...San Francisco
  Hal tead, James Lafayette, P. M. K. T......................   "
  Hart, Alfred...   "
  Holmes, Nathaniel Breed, 32°, K. T... ....Livermore
  Hackett, Henry..Grangeville
  Hewes, Charles Wesley, K. T......................................Oakland
  Haughton, Edward Wm...............................Valley View, Cramer
  Hurley, John, P. Th. Ill. M., K. T...............................Sacramento
  Hare, Elias, C., P. M..San Francisco
  Hanley, Wm. A., K. T...S. erra City

HAWKINS, EDWARD KENDRICK...San Francisco
*HADSELL, JAMES RICE..Monterey
HELLWIG, CHARLES J., 32°, P. M. P. H. P.............................Auburn
*HOBE, GEORGE JOHN, 33°, P. M. G. R.............................San Francisco
*HOSMER, HEZEKIAH P. M. K. T.......................................San Francisco
*HYDE, MARCUS DARIUS, P. M. R. A..................................Oakland
*HANDY, BRAYTON E., K. T...Oakland
*HULL, JOSEPH P. M...Sacramento
INGRAM, OSCAR S...San Diego
JENKINS, JOHN W., 32°, K. T..Nevada City
JOHNSON, ALBERT..Alameda
JOSSELYN, EDWARD SPENCER, K. T......................................Monterey
JONES, WILLIAM PRICE, K. T...Alameda
KING, WILLIAM AVERY, P. M..Oakland
KERCHIVAL, JOHN H., K. T..Oakland
KNORP, ALBERT FREDERICK, P. M. P. H. P.................San Francisco
KENNEDY, GEORGE EDWIN, 32° P. M. P. H. P. K. T.............Livermore
LANE, ANDREW JACKSON,...Knights Ferry
LAZZAREVICH, GIOVANNI, 32°, K. T.............................Los Angeles
LORD, CARLOS REUBEN, P. M. R. A....................................Berkeley
LAMPE, THEODORE C...San Francisco
LIPPMAN, GEORGE...   "
· LA BLANC, JOHN..   "
LENTELL, JAMES, P. M. P. H. P...Oakland
*LAWSON, JAMES S., 33°, R. A...San Francisco
McDONALD, RICHARD HAYES, K. T......................................   "
MERRITT, JAMES BESTOR, 33°, P. E. C. K. T...............Alameda County
MARTIN, JAMES C., P. M...Oakland
MACK, ALBERT...San Francisco
MAYER, LEOPOLD...   "
MASON, WM. C...Oakland
MILLER, PETER C., 32°..San Francisco
MERRILL, ISAAC M...San Diego
McGOUN, ROBERT., P. M. R. A...Alameda
MATHEWS, HENRY E., K T..San Francisco
McNERLY, MALACHI, 32°..Oakland
METCALF, GEORGE D., 32°, P. E. C. K. T.................................Oakland
*MOREL, ACHILLES, 33°..Fruitvale
McCLYMONDS JOHN WM., P. M. P. H. P. K. T.....................Oakland
*MIZNER, LANSING B., P. M..Benicia
*MULLARD, RICHARD T., 32°, P. M. K. T.........................Los Angeles
*McMILLAN, ROBERT, P. M..San Francisco
*MORGAN, EDWARD H., 32°, W. M. P. H. P. K. T..................Oakland
*NORTHEY, VERNAL SIDNEY...Oakland
OWENS, JOHN BROOME, P. M. K. T.............................. San Francisco
*OGILVIE, JAMES G., 18°..San Francisco
PHELPS, AUGUSTUS E..   "

PEARCE, RICHARD..Oakland
POWELL, ABRAHAM, 32°, P. M. K. T..................................   "
PEDRINI, CIPRIANO, K. T....................................North Temescal
PRESTON, ROBERT JAMES..Petaluma
PRICE, JOHN ASHLOCK..Orland
PATTERSON, GEORGE, 32°, K. T...................................   "
PHILLIPS, JOHN W., .K T...   "
PANNO, JOHN LEWIS..................................San Diego County
PATRICK, JOHN R., P. M...Monterey
PLUMMER, C. MOODY, 32° K. T....................San Francisco
PIERCE, WM. FRANK, 33°, P. H. P. T. I. G. M. K. T................Oakland
*PERRY, WM. H., 14° W. M.............................   "
*PARRISH, WM. H.......................................   "
*PRICE, WM. E., P. M.............................. ....San Francisco
RANDALL, BENJAMIN...................................Knights Ferry
RODOLPH, GODFREY, P. M. R. A..........................Madison
RODECKER, ELIAS, P. M.............................San Francisco
REISER, THEODORE, P. M. K. T.....................Anaheim
RUTHERFORD, CHARLES B., R. A............................Oakland
RIEGELHAUPT, PHILIP...............................San Francisco
ROSEKRANS, HENRY M...................................   "
RICE, HARVEY W..............................Haywards
REED, JOHN PITTS.....................................Coronado
SPAULDING, GEORGE, 32°, K. T......................San Francisco
SKINNER, ISAAC ASH, R. A..............................Monterey
STEWART, MICHAEL Y..................................Oakland
SHAW, SYLVANUS H., R. A...........................Sonoma
SOUTHER, JOSEPH N., 32°, K. T.....................San Francisco
SCHULLER, ANTONIO....................................Oakland
SIMPSON, ROBERT F...................................   "
*STANDEFORD, DAVID W..............................   "
SHAW, STEPHEN WM...............................San Francisco
STODDARD, ASA C................... ....Alameda
SUTTON, WM.....................................Monterey
*SWAIN, EDWARD B.................................San Francisco
*SMITH, JOSEPH C., P. M..... ....   "
*SAWYER, LORENZO D......................................   "
*SHURTLEFF, GEORGE. A., 32°, .KT...........................Napa
THOMPSON, ROBERT R.............................San Francisco
TERP, JEFF EVERSON.................................Oakland
TURNER, MATTHEW..............................San Francisco
TRULL, SYLVESTER, 32°, P. M..........................   "
*TAYLOR, JOHN B., 32°, K. T.............................Oakland
TOOTHAKER, LUTHER S................................Monterey
*TAYLOR, ROBERT H., P. M. R. A...................San Francisco
TILLEY, GABRIEL H....................................Oakland
VANDERSLICE, WM. K., K. T...........................   "

WILLIAMS, HENRY F., P. M., K. T., (First Mason made in Cal.)...S. F.
WINCHESTER, EBENEZER, 30°, P. M. R. A. R. S. M..............Oakland
WALTER, WM. ADDISON, P. M. R. A.......................... "
WRIGHT, WM. H., 30°, P. M. P. H. P.....................Livermore
WELLS, MICHAEL H., P. M. K. T.....................Yankee Hill
WINTERBURN, JOSEPH.....................San Francisco
WYNN, WATKYN WM.....................Livermore
WYTHE, REV. DR. JOSEPH M., 14°, P. G. O. K. T.....................Oakland
WOODRUFF, GEORGE J., K. T..................... "
*WILKINS, EDMUND T., 32°, K. T.....................Napa
WAGENER, SAMUEL HOPKINS, M. E. G. C. K. T.....................San Jose
*VANDERHURST, WILLIAM, P. G. H. P. K. T.....................Salinas
VAN PELT, JOHN HENRY.....................San Francisco
YERIAN, ADAM..................... "

OREGON.

M. W. G. M. CHRISTOPHER TAYLOR, 33°, P. G. H. P., P. Th.
G. M. P. G. C. K. T..............Dayton.
*M. W. P. G. M. JOHN C. AINSWORTH, 33°, K. T..........(Oakland, Cal.)
* " "   BENJAMIN STARK.....................———
* " "   JAMES R. BAYLEY, 32°.....................Newport
* " "   JOHN McCRAKEN, 33°.....................Portland
* " "   STEPHEN F. CHADWICK, 32°, K. T. Gr. Sec........Salem
* " "   A. W. FERGUSON.....................Astoria
* " "   DAVID G. CLARK.....................Albany
* " "   WILLIAM D. HARE ....———
* " "   THOMAS McF. PATTON, 32°, P. G. H. P. K. T.... Salem
* " "   J. H. KUNZIE.....................———
* " "   ROBERT CLOW.....................———
* " "   ROCKY P. EARHART, 33°, P. G. H. P. G. C. K. T.———
* " "   GEORGE McD. STROUD.....................———
* " "   JOSEPH N. DOLPH, 33°, K. T..................... ....Portland
* " "   WILLIAM T. WRIGHT, 32°.....................Union
* " "   D. P. MASON..................... ... .———
* " "   THOMAS G. REAMES, 32°, K. T..................Jacksonville
* " "   JAMES C. FULLERTON ....———
* " "   ANDREW NASBURY, 32°, K. T.....................Marshfield
* " "   JAMES F. ROBINSON.....................Eugene City
* " "   G. M. JACOB MAYER.....................Portland
*V. W. P. G. Sec. FRELON J. BABCOCK, 32°, K. T.....................Salem
V. W. P. G. I. Sec. IRVING W. PRATT, 33°, P. H. P. P. A. C. K. T.
Portland

JAMES W. COOK, 32°, K. T..................... "
*W. ROBERT P. BIRD, P. M.....................Lafayette

WASHINGTON.

*M. W. P. G. M. LOUIS ZIEGLER, 33°, G. H. P., Vice-Pres. for Wash.
Spokane Falls

*M. W. P. G. M. Daniel Bagley...Seattle
*   "   "   Elwood Evans, 32°...Tacoma
*   "   "   Granville O. Haller, 32°...........................Seattle
*   "   "   James R. Hayden, 33°......./............................ "
*   "   "   Platt A. Preston, 32°..............................Waitsburg
*   "   "   Robert C. Hill, 32°..........................Port Townsend
*   "   "   Elisha P. Ferry, 32°...................................Seattle
*   "   "   Louis Sohns, 32°.......................................Vancouver
*   "   "   Ralph Guichard, 32°..........................Walla Walla
*   "   "   Joseph A. Kuhn, 32°.........................Port Townsend
*   "   "   Levi Ankeny, 32°...........................Walla Walla
*   "   "   William H. White ....Seattle
*   "   "   Joseph Smith.......................................Kalama
*   "   "   Nathan S. Potter, 32°...............................Olympia
*   "   "   Hanford W. Fitzweather, 32°...................Sprague
*   "   "   P. S. Admiston..Ellensburg
*   "   "   Thomas M. Reed, 33°, Gr. Sec., G. R. K. T....Olympia
*R. W. P. G. S. W., John Webster, 32° (18)............................Seattle

NEVADA.

W. Alexander D. Rock, R. A., Vice-President........................Eureka
*M. W. P. G. M. Joseph de Bell, 32°........................(Oakland, Cal.)
*   "   "   Robert W. Bollen, 32°..........................(Elsinore.)
*   "   "   Horatio S. Mason..........................(Murrietta, Cal.)
*   "   "   Michael A. Murphy...........................Carson City
*   "   "   Henry Rolfe.....................................Virginia City
   "   "   Adolph L. Fitzgerald, 33°, P. G. H. P.........Eureka
*   "   "   Andrew Nichols, K. T...............(Los Angeles, Cal.)
*   "   "   Merrill P. Freeman, 33°, (Also P. G. M. and
                                        G. S. of Arizona, Tucson)
*   "   "   David E. Barley...........................(San Diego, Cal.)
*   "   "   Henry L. Fish..Reno
*   "   "   William McMillan...........................Virginia City
*   "   "   Charles W. Hinchcliff...............................Austin
*   "   G. M.   John W. Eckley...................................Virginia City
*V. W. G. S.   Chauncey N. Noteware, R. A...............Carson City
   "   P. "   Samuel W. Chubbuck, K, T...............(Oakland, Cal.)
*   "   "   Robert H. Taylor, K. T............(San Francisco, Cal.)
W. Daniel W. Levan, 32°..Eureka
W. Joseph R. Kendall, W. M. K. T ....Hamilton
W. Fletcher H. Harmon, 33°, P. M., (20) ....Eureka

IDAHO.

*M. W. P. G. M. Jonas W. Browne..................................Boise City
*   "   "   John Kenally.......................................Idaho City
*   "   "   Edward A. Stevenson..............................Boise City
*   "   "   Charles Himrod.................................. "
*   "   "   Francis E. Ensign....................................Hailey
*   "   "   La Fayette Carter....................................Boise City

*M. W. P. G. M. GEORGE H. DAVIS..................................Boise City
*   "   "   JOHN HUNTER..   "
*   "   "   CHESTER P. COBURN, 32°...........................Lewiston
*   "   "   GEORGE L. SHARP.................................Boise City
*V. W. G. Sec. JAMES H. WICKERSHAM, (11)...................—   "

MONTANA.

M. W. P. G. M., HARRY R. COMELY, 33°, K. T., Vice President, Helena
*   "   "   JOHN J. HULL..——
*   "   "   LEANDER W. FRARY.................................——
*   "   "   WEBBER F. SANDERS..............................Helena
*   "   "   NATH. P. SANFORD................................——
*   "   "   CORNELIUS HEDGES, 33°, Gr. Sec...............Helena
*   "   "   JAMES R. WESTON................................Townsend
*   "   "   JAMES R. BOYCE, Sr................................Butte
*   "   "   SOL. STARR...Helena
*   "   "   EDWARD S. STACKPOLE.........................Deer Lodge
*   "   "   JULIAN M. KNIGHT.........................Virginia City
*   "   "   WM. A. CLARKE...............................Deer Lodge
*   "   "   JOHN STEADMAN....................................Helena
*   "   "   HIRAM KNOWLES.............................Deer Lodge
*   "   "   GEORGE W. MONROE.............................Bozeman
*   "   "   THOMAS H. POMEROY.........................Missoula
*   "   "   ANSOLEM J. DAVIDSON.........................Helena
*   "   "   HUGH DUNCAN....................................Sheridan
*   "   "   S. W. LANGSHORNE.............................Bozeman
*   "   "   JOSEPH A. HYDE, 32°...............................Butte
*   "   "   SAMUEL WORD.............................Virginia City
*   "   "   JAMES W. HATHAWAY........................Helena
*   "   "   ARTHUR C. LOGAN(23)........................Miles City

WYOMING.

*M. W. P. G. M. N. R. DAVIS....................................Cheyenne
*   "   "   WILLIAM DAILEY.................................Rawlins
*   "   "   J. H. HAYFORD....................................——
*   "   "   ROBERT WILSON..................................——
*   "   "   E. P. SNOW...——
*   "   "   J. K. JEFFREY.....................................——
*   "   "   F. F. WILLIAMS...................................——
*   "   "   F. E. ADAMS..——
*   "   "   F. C. ADDOMS, K. T...........................Cheyenne
*   "   "   WM. H. FOOTE, 33°.............................Evanston
*   "   "   E. F. CHENEY..Lander
*   "   "   L. S. BARNES.......................................Laramie
*V. W. G. Sec. WM. L. KUYKENDALL (13)................Cheyenne

COLORADO.

M. W. P. G. M. LAWRENCE N. GREENLEAF, 33°, K. T. Vice-Pres..Denver
*   "   "   JOHN M. CHIVINGTON.........................   "

*M. W. P. G. M. Henry M. Teller, 33°...............................Denver
* " " Archibald J. VanDus n.............................. "
* " " Webster D. Anthony............................. "
* " " Oren H. Henry.................................. "
* " " Harper M. Orahood.............................. "
* " " Cornelius J. Hart.....................Pueblo
* " " Roger W. Woodbury, 16°.................Denver
* " " Byron L. Carr.................................. "
* " " Robert A. Quillian........................... "
* " " Frank Church.............................. "
* " " Andrew Sagendorf.................Cheyenne
* " " James H. Peabody, G. C. K. T.............Cañon City
* " " William D. Todd...........................Denver
* " " George E. Wyman...........................Longmont
* " " Albert H. Branch.........................Denver
* " " George H. Kimball........................Golden
* " " Wm. T. Brilwell.........................Denver
V. W. G. S., Edward C. Parmelee, 33°, G R. K. T.............Pueblo
V. W. G. M. Henry Trucy West, (22)..........................Greeley

Utah.

*M. W. P. G. M. James Lowe, 32°, E. C. K. T., Vice-President,
                                                Salt Lake City
* " " Louis Cohn................................. " "
* " " Charles W. Bennett........................ " "
* " " Edward P. Johnson......................... ——
* " " John Show Scott, G. T................Salt Lake City
* " " Thomas E. Clohecy......................... " "
* " " William F. James.......................... " "
* " " Parley L. Williams........................ " "
* " " Samuel Paul............................... " "
* " " Albert R. Heywood.......................Ogden
* " " Arthur M. Grant.......................Salt Lake City
*V. W. G. Sec., Christopher Diehl (12)................... " "

Arizona.

W. Alex. G. Oliver, P. M. G. H. P. K. T. Vice President.. Fort Whipple
*M. W. P. G. M. Francis A. Shaw, K. T......................Phœnix
* " " Martin W. Kales, 32°, K. T....................... "
* " " Ansel M. Bragg, 32, R. A...........(Los Angeles, Cal.)
* " " Benjamin Titus, 14°...........(Lordsburg, New Mexico)
* " " Merrill P. Freeman, 33°, G. S. K. T.
                (P. G. M also of Nevada)...........Tucson
* " " Morris Goldwater, R. A......................Prescott
* " " George J. Roskrug, 32°, K. T., (8)..............Tuscon

New Mexico.

W. Joseph V. Cowan, W. M., Vice President................Kingston
*M. W. P. G. M. William W. Griffin, 32°........................ Santa Fe
* " " Samuel B. Newcomb, 32°.................... "
* " ' John B Wooten......................... ——
* ' " Wm. L. Revnerson, 32........ .... Santa Fe
* " " Henry M. Walds, 32°.................... "
* " " Wm. B. Chiiders, 32° .... "
* " " Cornelius W. Bennett......................——
* " " Max Frost, 32°........................Santa Fe
* " " W. S. Harroun, 32° ... . "
* " " Alex. H. Morhead, K. T...............Silver City
*V. W. G. Sec. Alpheus A. Keen.....................Los Vegas
V. W. Westy Petersen, (13) ....Kingston

BRITISH COLUMBIA.

*M. W. P. G. M. ISRAEL W. POWELL.....................................Victoria
* " " SIMEON DUCK.................................. "
* " " FREDERICK WILLIAMS .... "
* " " ELI HARRI ON, Sr. R. A............................ "
* " " HENRY BROWN, Gr. Sec............................ "
* " " EDGAR C. BAKER................................. "
* " " THOMAS TROUNCE .... "
* " " WILLIAM DALBY................................. "
* " " ALEX. R. MILNE............................... "
* " " H. E. HEISTERMAN, G. T...................... "
*V. W. P. G. Sec. EDWARD S. NEWFELDER (11)..................... "

Honorary Members Elsewhere.

MASSACHUSETTS.

*BENJAMIN DEAN, 33°, P. G. M. K. T. U. S.............................Boston
*EDWIN B. SPINNEY, 14°, K. T., Corr. Sec............................... "

MARYLAND.

*W. WM. E. STEUART, Corr. Sec......................................Baltimore

DISTRICT OF COLUMBIA.

*ALBERT PIKE, 33°, Grand Com. Sup. Con. S. J. U. S. A......Washington
*FRED. WEBBER, 33°, Sec. Gen. Corr. Sec......................... "
*PHILIP HICHBORN, 32°, Naval Constructor, U. S. N............ "

VIRGINIA.

*ROBERT A. WITHERS, 33°, P. G. M. K. T. U. S....................Richmond

IOWA.

*THEODORE S. PARVIN, 33°, P. G. M. P. G. Rec. K. T. U. S...Cedar Rapids

LOUISIANA.

*M. W. P. G. M. JOHN Q. A. FELLOWS, 33°, P. G. M. K. T. U. S.,
New Orleans
* " " SAMUEL M. TODD, 33°, K. T..................... "
* " " JAMES C. BATCHELOR, 33°, Lt. Gr. Com.
Sup. Con. S. J. U. S. Gr. Sec. Corr. Sec...................... "
*RICHARD LAMBERT, 32°, Asst. Gr. Sec. .... "

* Honorary Members.

OFFICERS

OF THE

𝔑ational 𝔠onvention

OF

ℳasonic 𝒱eteran 𝒜ssociations

OF THE

UNITED STATES.

Organized Wednesday Evening, October 9th, 1889, at the Scottish Rite Sanctuary, corner of Third and E Streets, Washington City, D. C.

PAST PRESIDENT.

ALBERT PIKE,...Washington City, D. C.

PRESIDENT.

CHARLES E. MEYER,...Philadelphia

VICE-PRESIDENTS.

THEOPHILUS PRATT, for the Atlantic Division.................New York City
LA FAYETTE VAN CLEVE, for the East Mississippi Division, Cincinnati, O.
THEODORE S. PARVIN, for the West Mississippi Division, Cedar Rapids, Ia.
EDWIN A. SHERMAN, for the Pacific Division.....................Oakland, Cal.

SECRETARY.

GEORGE H. FISH..New York City, New York

TREASURER.

A. T. LONGLEY,..Washington City, D. C.

The Masons on the Mountains.

[FROM THE VIRGINIA (NEV.) TERRITORIAL ENTERPRISE, SEPT. 9, 1875.]

The Meeting of Virginia Lodge, No. 3, upon the Top of Mt. Davidson — The Highest Lodge ever opened in the United States, if not in the World — The Cause of the Unusual Proceeding—The Improvised Altar, Chairs, Etc.—The Doings, Speeches, Attendance, Etc., Etc.

The world has existed so long that it is difficult to do anything that never was done before. If it be true as alleged, that history repeats itself, it must be equally true that the actions of men are repeated, for the record of these constitute the history of the world. In this turning over of the doings of the world, whereby the transactions of former years, when the world was young, are brought again, by the revolving centuries, to the summit of action, so as to appear startling and new, it is fitting that a land like ours, freshly won from the scenes of nature, should be the field of that action. The world was young in the arts, sciences and civilization, if not in years, when they were first enacted, and it is eminently proper that they should be reproduced in a land where civilization is a recent importation, and where the surroundings are counterparts of those which existed in those far-off years.

A STEP IN THE REPEATING HISTORY OF THE WORLD

Was taken by "Virginia Lodge, No. 3, of Free and Accepted Masons" yesterday, and a cycle in the history of the world was completed. By the burning up of the Masonic Hall in this city last May, the Brethren were deprived of their place of meeting. They were then, with others similarly situated, invited to the Odd Fellows Hall, and were glad to accept of the courtesies then tendered them. When by the destructive fire of last Friday morning, they were again deprived, with their benefactors and others, of a place where they might congregate, and found themselves, as were many of their ancient brethren in the early days of Masonry, without a place of meeting it occurred to them to imitate those early patrons of the art; and as their ancient brethren were wont to hold their meetings on the tops of high hills or in low valleys, they resolved to hold

A LODGE UPON THE MOUNTAIN TOP.

The place of meeting was certainly the strangest one of modern days. The brethren of the present day are accustomed to hold their communications in the upper chambers, for the better security there afforded, but here was an instance where an original custom was to be wedded to an original rite. The custom of meeting upon high hills, grew naturally out of the practice of the early Jews, who built their temples, schools and synagogues in conspicuous places. This seems to have met in those early days with the approbation of the Almighty, for we read in Ezekiel where he said: "Upon the top of the mountain, the whole limit thereof, shall be most holy." Before the erection of temples even, celestial bodies were worshipped on hills, and terrestrial ones in valleys. The early Christians, whenever it was practicable, erected their churches on eminences.

THE TOP OF MOUNT DAVIDSON

Is by actual measurement, seven thousand eight hundred and twenty-seven feet above the level of the sea. The apex from which the flag-staff rises, is one thousand six hundred and twenty-two feet above the level of B Street, corner of Taylor. The summit is three thousand five hundred feet west of the city, so that in a straight line from B street, corner of Taylor, to the foot of the flag-staff, it is a little over three thousand eight hundred and fifty-seven feet, or not far from three-quarters of a mile. But by the traveled route, the distance is long and tedious.

Footmen can go direct over the track run by the racers. Horse and foot can pass through Taylor street and Taylor Ravine to the ridge, and thence to the summit. "Bullion Ravine" is passable for horsemen, by skirting the eastern base of the mountain and winding to the west of the peak. Besides these, there is the route by the way of the Ophir grade to the top of the ridge, to the west, and thence back east to the top. This is the route by which the most of the carriages made the summit yesterday.

THE LODGE.

Never since the morning stars sang their lullaby over the cradled earth was there a more perfect representation of a Masonic lodge-room, than the one in which the members of "Virginia, No. 3," and their visiting brethren held communication yesterday. This existed not only in the Charter, the Greater and the Lesser Lights, and the number requisite to compose a Lodge, but it was literally bounded but by the extreme points of the compass. Its dimensions from east to west, embraced every clime from north to south. Its covering was no less than the clouded canopy ; and it is only where this is wanting that the literal supports, the three great pillars of Wisdom, Strength and Beauty are needed. But metaphorically, they were all there, for where in a lodge-room, was ever seen such wisdom to contrive, strength to support and beauty to adorn? Verily it was a meeting in the Temple of Deity, and the wisdom, strength and beauty which are about His throne, were present in the symmetry, order and grandeur of this primitive lodge room. It was a lodge the dimensions of which, like the universal chain of the Order, included the entire human family. Upon the brow of the mountain, and a little south of the flag-staff,

AN ALTAR OF ROUGH ASHLARS

Had been improvised, whereon rested the Three Great Lights of Masonry. Beside them stood the representatives of the Three Lesser Lights. Rude chairs had also been built of rough granite for the Worshipful Master, Senior and Junior Wardens, while the Deacons found ample accommodation among the boulders around. A large "G" had been cut from sheet metal and nailed to the flag-staff. The Tyler was indeed in trouble, for in such a place how could the lodge be duly tyled in accordance with modern usage. But under the direction of the Worshipful Master, a line of pickets, designated by white badges on their left arms, were stationed all around the brow of the summit. They were near each other, so that none could pass or re-pass without permission. In that way the approach of cowans and eaves-droppers was effectually guarded against. On reaching the summit, the brethren busied themselves with dispensing and partaking of

CORN, WINE AND OIL.

A bounteous collation had been prepared by the Lodge, and members were mostly well provided with the means of refreshments, nourishment and joy. These were dispensed with a liberal hand. All were welcome and partook with an appetite sharpened by the labor of the ascent and the fresh air, which swept the summit with a freedom known only to Washoe zephyrs. While all this was going on, the members of "Virginia Lodge, No. 3," and visiting brethren were engaged in registering their names.

Instead of the regular Lodge register, large sheets of drawing paper had been prepared to receive the signatures, with a view to framing them and hanging them among the adornments of their lodge-room when it is ready for dedication. This work of obtaining the names of those present took upward of two hours. At length, the hour of opening having arrived,

THE CRAFT WAS CALLED FROM REFRESMENT TO LABOR

By the sounding of the gavel in the East. The task of clothing was also a tedious one. Ample provision had been made for this, but some of the brethren were compelled to improvise the emblem of innocence and badge of a Mason by making a white apron of their pocket handkerchiefs. It was found however, to be impracticable to satisfy the presiding officer that all present were Master Masons, and a special dispensation granted by Robert W. Bollen, Most Worshipful Grand Master of Nevada, that the lodge be opened then and there without form, for the regular transaction of business. The opening ode was therefore sung by the lodge quartet, composed of Professor E. Pasmore, George N. Eells, C. L. Foster and George W. Dorwin, a brief prayer was offered up by Rev. G. D. Hammond, and the white Masonic flag, more ancient than the Golden Fleece or Roman Eagle, for the first time in the history of the world, displayed from the top of Mt. Davidson. As the wind unwrapped its folds and displayed the square, compass and letter G emblazoned thereon, it was greeted with three cheers and a tiger that must have been heard for miles around.

THE LODGE WAS THEN DECLARED DULY OPENED.

The following officers being present—to wit:

ALBERT HIRES.. *Worshipful Master*
ALEXANDER DUNN..*Senior Warden*
CHARLES HARPER..*Junior Warden*
GEORGE H. DANA..*Treasurer*
G. F. FORD...*Secretary*
PHILIP SELDNER...*Senior Deacon*
JOHN CAMERON...*Junior Deacon*
JOHN FARNSWORTH }
W. P. BLIGHT   } ....*Stewards*
J. A. McQUARRIE...*Marshal*
C. L. FISHER..*Chaplain*
E. J. PASMORE..*Organist*
E. S. KINCAID..*Tyler*
THOMAS P. JONES, E. CHAMBERLAIN, ALEXANDER G. COWAN, JAMES W. SILL, JOHN ABBOTT, WILLIAM J. McMILLAN, DAVID L. JONES, G. W. ROBERTSON, J. H. DYER and T. X. GOYETTE

Sentinels

It will not be amiss in this connection to state that

THE JEWELS WORN

By the officers of the Lodge have just been subjected to a fiery ordeal. They were made of Ophir Bullion in the year 1863, at the order of the late Colonel W. H. Howard and by him presented to the Lodge. Their cost was $500. They were saved from the destruction which laid waste the Masonic Hall in the early summer, but the fire of last Friday morning found them in the hall of the Odd Fellows where the Lodge met after being burned out. They were mourned over as lost, but were finally dug out of the ashes nearly perfect, but a single one being missing. Some of those recovered have had portions melted away, but there is enough left to show the original design and to carry the identity on down to future generations. There were also present at the opening, the following

GRAND OFFICERS.

ROBERT W. BOLLEN...*M. W. Grand Master*
J. M. McGINNIS...*W. Grand Marsha*

PAST GRAND OFFICERS.

J. C. CURRIE   }
G. W. HOPKINS }..*Past Grand Masters*
R. T. MULLARD..*Past Deputy Grand Master*
C. F. BRANT ....*Past Senior Grand Warden*
R. H. TAYLOR...*Past Grand Secretary*

The Lodge being informally opened, several ladies who had made the ascent were admitted, as were also several children, among them two of the Hon. C. E. De Long, together with their Japanese attendant.

Past Grand Master J. C. Currie then introduced Robert W. Bollen, Most Worshipful Grand Master of Nevada, who was invited by the Master to accept the chair and preside over the Lodge. The invitation was accepted. In taking the chair, the Most Worshipful Grand Master thanked the Brethren for the honor conferred upon him. He had been twenty-eight years a member of the fraternity but that was the happiest moment of his life. He then alluded to the custom of the ancient brethren to meet on high hills or in low valleys. "Virginia Lodge No. 3," had ascended the mountain and given rise to the great occasion by opening a lodge higher than any opened in the United States.

The Grand Master then gave accounts of some preliminary meetings which have been held on the Coast on the top of the hills. He spoke of one near Ragtown, where the brethren had come together in that way to raise money and provisions for suffering immigrants, and over which he had the honor to preside. He also mentioned a similar gathering in Eureka, in 1851, and at Auburn, California. He also gave the account of another preliminary meeting held in that way, when the first three degrees ever conferred in the lodge were conferred on a hill.

But none of these were gatherings like the present, and he thanked the Brethren that he had been called upon to preside over their deliberations.

The Lodge being opened for the transaction of business, a petition was read, received and referred.

A communication was also presented, in which Bishop Whitaker offered to the Lodge the use of the school room belonging to St. Paul's Church, in which to meet. The communciation was ordered on file and the thanks of the Lodge tendered in return.

Bills were presented and referred.

J. C. Currie of the Committee on Resolutions in regard to the death of Brother Thomas Sheehan presented his report.

This closed the regular order of business. Under the head "The good of Masonry,"

THE HON. C. E. DE LONG

was called for and responded very happily—the following brief sketch of his remarks not doing him justice:

He had only just been apprised of the fact that the Brother who was expected to talk to the Brethren was not present. Mr. De Long alluded to the fact that events however unimportant in themselves, and considered trifling at the time, not unfrequently marked great epochs in the world's history. The events of the day, although considered but the events of a holiday, would be a marked epoch in Masonry. The speaker pictured forcibly the rise and fall of nations. It was the pride and glory of the Craft that it had survived the fall of governments and all the changes of the moving world.

They were assembled beneath the all-seeing eye of Him who is the Grand Architect of the Universe, and it behooved each brother with that light shining into his heart, to ask himself if he was living true to the tenets of the Order, and to the lessons taught in the lodge-room.

Mr. I eLong sketched the surroundings within which they had erected their altar. Beneath them was the wealth of Ophir, and around them the tumult of trade. The earth seemed cursed and rendered an unfit dwelling place for man, but it was to be redeemed through the intelligence of man, and each had a part to perform in the work. The speaker told how in Japan he had assisted in welding the link in Masonry which made the chain complete around the world. Up to that time, there had been one land where the Order was not known. Now there was none. Masonry belted the globe. The lights of the altar had been lighted, and now there were six lodges in the Empire and the Order was rapidly spreading.

Colonel R. H. Taylor was then called for, and responded by reading the following poem:

> The Lord unto the Prophet said,
> "Upon the mountain's topmost round,
> Far as the breezy limits spread,
> Shall be most holy ground."
>
> 'Neath God's blue dome on lofty hills
> Whose crests first catch the morning heat—
> Whose hights the evening glory fills—
> The Craft was wont to meet.
>
> There, far above the busy mart,
> And from its care and turmoil free,
> They learned the lessons of the heart
> To "work" and to "agree."
>
> Oh, sacred hills of olden time,
> Whose hoary crags resist the gale,
> Ye have a history sublime
> That ages cannot pale.
>
> Again to-day, the sons of light,
> As did their sires of olden days,
> Upon the mountain's dizzy hight,
> Their mystic banner raise.
>
> Again above the busy marts,
> Where human feet have seldom trod,
> We raise our voices and our hearts
> In reverence to God.
>
> Almighty Father! by whose will
> The mountains rise and worlds do move,
> Thy blessings grant, descend and fill
> Each Mason's heart with love.

Mr. Edwin A. Sherman was called out and spoke briefly to the point. He recounted instances in the early days of California when the brethren met on hills. It was a peculiar and significant circumstance that to-day they were assembled around the summit of Mount Davidson. David's son was Solomon, our Most Ancient Grand Master.

The speaker spoke of the three first lodges established in California and their uniting in establishing the Grand Lodge of that State, the parent of Virginia Lodge No. 3, which had that day consecrated the top of the mountain as their lodge room.

A speech was made by General Williams, in which the past of some of the members of the Order were graphically and feelingly sketched. R. M. Daggett, after repeated calls, responded by taking out his watch and carefully noting the time. It was 4:30 o'clock. It would take him an hour and a half to get down. He made his point, and brought his remarks to a close by saying, "I have nothing against any brother here, so help me God!"

Messrs Currie and Hopkins were called out, and responded briefly. The point of Brother Daggett's remarks had cut short all long-winded speeches, if any had been contemplated.

On motion of Mr. DeLong, a vote of thanks was tendered to General J. B. Winter, for starting the movement which had resulted in the meeting on the mountain.

A touching prayer was then offered by Rev. S. P. Kelly. "Old Lang Syne" was sung in full chorus by all present, and the lodge was then declared closed in ample form.

The register showed the following

MEMBERS OF VIRGINIA LODGE, No. 3.

E. Strother,	J. E. Terp,	J. P. Smith,
L. H. Torp,	Colin L. Foster,	R. Andrews,
Thomas Cooper, •	C. L. Fisher,	Alex. Dunn,
James Singleton,	Henry Piper,	T. H. Goyette,
M. J. Henley,	Wm. Maver,	J. P. Hutchinson,
A. V. Comstock,	Wm. B. Hickok,	A. J. Wren,
H. P Kearns,	B. M. Townsend,	F. Martell,
C. M. Laurence,	B. Galligan,	F. M. Thayer,
John T. Hambly,	J. R. Wood,	L. Rawlings,
Benj. Williams,	Robert Laird,	John C. Lillie,
Edward Cox,	Theodore Wolff,	John S. Ryno,
D. L. Jones,	Samuel Platt,	S. B. Legur,
A. B. C. Davis,	M. E. Glover,	H. S. Beck,
William Brown,	Jacob Morris,	M. Mygatt,
E. Jackson,	Wm. McMillan,	John Abbott,
J. W. Hemenway,	John Evans,	J. D. De St. Croix,
George W. Dorwin,	C. E. DeLong,	Wm. J. Smyth,
V. Jones,	Lee McGown,	R. Andrews,
Wales Averill,	J. W. Booth,	Mark Brown,
R. M. Daggett,	J. H. Dyer,	Benj. P. Smith,
F. C. Bishop,	William Box,	G. Stevens, .
T. M. Adams,	Wm. R. King,	W. G. Thompson,
G W. Hammer,	John Evans.	'

VISITING BRETHREN.

F. C. Lord,	G. F. Hayward,	J. C. Laurence,
T. H. Flagler,	A. J. Banker,	I. M. Thaxton,
E. Chamberlin,	I. S. Burson,	Alfred Troude,
J. M. Hickman,	J. B. Conrad,	D. Edmonds,
H. Donnelly,	G. W. Cook,	T. H. Whister,
E. M. Long,	J. S. Adams,	Joseph Guess,
R. S. Bromley,	Henry Lux,	Thos. Morrison,
A. Clark,	J. S. Coxter,	E. S. Benner,
J. B. Braslau,	J. J. Alexander,	John B. Winters,
E. A. SHERMAN, .	D. Harrington,	H. A. Clawson,
Wm. Collicutt,	D. W. McIntosh,	G. H. McKey,
Wm. M. Laforce,	M. Banner,	Wm. Wallace,
J. H. Molkembahr,	A. T. Hampton,	George W. Hopkins,
A. L. Murphy,	D. Skerry,	R. H. Taylor,
G. W. Robertson,	H. J. T. Scheel,	Sam. Owen,
G. H. Winterburn,	D. McNaught,	L. Lobenstein,
A. M. Kruttschmitt,	R. Baird,	A. D. Ritchof,
Wm. Nelson,	T. A. Atkinson,	S. J. Blair,
George Faull,	J. R. Cowan,	Prosper Bruley,
J. D. Hammond,	C. W. Toger,	T. Deignau,
I. Z. Kelley,	W. McKeighan,	J. McCain,
T. McGovern,	Bob. Marshall,	Wm. McCrum,
Paul Jones, .	John J. Oswald,	J. F. Lewis,
A. Thompson,	F. V. Drake,	W. W. Dunlap,
S. P. Kelley,	J. H. Heilshorn,	Wilson King,
J. Wellington,	M. A. Macdonald,	T. Tully,
Wm. J. Pendray,	J. D. Horking,	W. H. Kneebone,
J. Chegwidden,	J. S. Ingraham,	S. J. Walker,

A. G. Cowan,
Henry Tonkin,
E. D. Williams,
J. G. McKenzie,
Joseph Sparks,
John Lentz,
Wm. Avery,
John Riley,
Edw. Conradt,
H. Falk,
W. J. Williams,
Charles V. Boisot,
A. H. W. Creigh,
L. O. Templeton,
George S. Johnson,
I. F. Berry,
B. H. Lentz,
Peter Turnob,
John Canning,
G. W. Hammond,
W. H. Mitchell,
William Mill,
Charles Glover,
John Wilson,
John R. Lowe,
E. W. Adams,
H. M. Cameron,
W. D. Sutherlin,
J. W. Van Zandt,
Paul T. Kirby,
J. D. Weddorf,
J. D. Delsort,
O. B. McDonald,
John Hewitt,
S. W. Grant,
W. W. Filkins,
Hugh Halligan,
S. Zenovich,
Jas. Chegwidden,
E. Bloomfield,
F. H. Packer,
Wm. Vardy,
Joseph Agortini,
H. O. Smith,
A. D. Praxnin,
J. D. Kenney,
G. N. Eells,
John B. Fegan,
L. G. Chapman,
Edwin Frolick,
John Cauble,
Thos. Frellian,
James Ryan,
Jos. Cornelius,
J. P. Rugg,
John Deman,
R. Brown,
George Clark,
Adam Gunn,

C. F. Brant,
D. Springsted,
M. W. Hassett,
T. H. Williams,
R. J. Peters,
John Horking,
Joseph Mitchell,
P. J. Aiken,
W. J. Westerfield,
Thos. Penrose,
Ananias May,
J. B. Shay,
W. F. Alexander,
A. L. Murphy,
J. B. Marshall,
J. H. Ellsworth,
A. J. Banker,
Evan David,
Sam. P. Kelly,
John H. Shermieo,
J. C. Turner,
J. R. Jacoby,
Robert Thomas,
J. H. Hubbs,
E. R. Edge,
S. B. Ferguson,
Frank D. Turner,
S. B. Connor,
F. F. Osbiston,
Chas. F. Hoffman,
John H. Britman,
S. N. Snyder,
E. D. Williams,
Simon Davis,
James Jewell,
E. D. Kitzmeyer,
T. W. McCready,
Wm. Garhart,
Richard Cook,
Robert Hayes,
Wm. L. Ames,
Jacob Waite,
Albert Werner,
Joseph Halleck,
John Chapman,
Charles Thompson,
Geo. L. Porter,
Geo. B. Allen,
C. A. Washington,
S. Longabaugh,
J. A. Hoher,
B. J. Wakefield,
S. T. Leebes,
J. W. Sill,
C. C. McLaughlin,
W. A. Perkins,
Desiro Rerieo,
J. C. Bebcher,
W. H. Gidlow,

H. B. Fay,
J. Portman,
H. C. Jacobson,
W. P. Workley,
N. C. Kinney,
Alex. Picken,
J. H. Matthewson,
B. I. Turman,
Wm. Webber,
Geo. B. McLean,
Robert Keifer,
L. M. Coffin,
E. Mortensen,
George Duprey,
Sam. H. Birtle,
Wm. Erskin,
J. Oates,
Wm. H. Bennetts,
James Parker,
Thomas E. Jones,
R. M. Elliott,
C. H. Golding,
Sol. Noel,
G. D. Kend,
A. H. Hollister,
J. C. Coulter,
Matthew Elliott,
D. S. Dow,
Horatio Collins,
John T. Reardon,
Wm. H. Cloud,
Geo. W. Williams,
A. C. Freeman,
James P. Nelson,
O. Lavigne,
D. D. Donovan,
C. S. Mott,
J. M. Campbell,
Peter Daley,
George Rook,
C. N. Collins,
D. Stalker,
John T. Brey,
Henry Faull,
E. P. Lovejoy,
B. Benson,
R. W. Guild,
W. H. Curnon,
Thomas Farsen,
George H. Warren,
E. B. Stonehill,
H. B. Loomis,
R. G. Westerman,
George Keightley,
Henry Rolfo,
Peter Frost,
John G. Young,
J. H. Bartlett,
W. D. Husk,

R. A. Bulm,	James Lynch,	T. J. Hodgkinson,
John F. Perry,	James Morris,	Henry Green,
L. C. Wiggins,	J. C. McDonald,	Wm. Sutherland,
W. H. Smith,	Fred Harper,	J. D. Dessert,
E. H. Jeffs,	R. M. G. Stewart,	Richard Saiu,
Boaz D. Pike,	W. Whittley,	John Carpenter,
James Bullen,	S. H. Goddard,	Wm. Trounce.

By the visitors named above were the following

STATES AND COUNTRIES REPRESENTED:

New York, California, West Virginia, Kansas, Michigan, Utah, Missouri, Iowa, Wisconsin, Maine, Colorado, New Jersey, Washington, District of Columbia, England, Scotland, Minnesota, Massachusetts, Oregon, Washington Territory, Virginia, Nova Scotia, North Carolina, Nebraska, Pennsylvania, Illinois, Canada West, Idaho, New Zealand and Kentucky.

UP AND DOWN AND MOUNTAIN.

The members of the Masonic Fraternity, presented a fantastic appearance as they gathered and started for the top of Mount Davidson, yesterday. About seven o'clock in the morning a commissary wagon was sent up by the Ophir grade. At eleven o'clock the teams began to collect their loads and go. The vehicles were not allowed to run light, every nook and corner being crammed with something satisfying to the demands of the inner man. Then came the footman and the equestrians. From that hour till two P. M., groups could be seen on foot and horseback going for the hights, and at all points, intermediate between the city and flag-staff. By the aid of the glasses on the top, the anxious gazers in Virginia City and Gold Hill were plainly discernable. When the exercises were closed, a regular scamper commenced down the mountain. Most came down by Taylor ravine, some by Bullion ravine and not a few enjoyed the beautiful ride over the Orphir grade. Taken altogether, it was a remarkable day. Very few mishaps were experienced in going up and down the mountain. Occasionally, a bottle of water would come in contact with a stone and the contents be lost, and wrecks of unappropriated lunches were not unfrequently encountered on the way down. But no serious accident occurred, and all seemed happy in the event and contented with the result. Those who participated have a rare experience, which will yield them a life-long satisfaction.

The multitude yesterday upon the mountain, were greatly indebted to Mr. Mackey for the thoughtful and timely donation of one hundred and fifty pounds of ice, which he hired toted to the top, on the backs of two Chinamens' mules. These mules were afterwards stationed between the flag-staff and the city, and may have been mistaken by near-sighted individuals for true Masonic goats.

MASONIC BUILDING ASSOCIATION.

Before the members of the Masonic fraternity were called to order yesterday, Mayor Currie and Secretary Hopkins invited those wishing to come forward and subscribe to the capital stock of the Masonic Building Association. The brethren responded quite liberally, considering the times. Many of them had already subscribed, and the others took about seven hundred shares yesterday. There are but two thousand shares in all. Forty per cent. of the subscription will be called for about the first of October, and then the balance will be paid in installments. The stock will pay from one to one and a half per cent. per month. It is the intention of the Trustees to have the building ready to be occupied by January first.

RELIC SEEKERS.

The gathering yesterday around the flag-staff on the top of Mount Davidson was not without its characteristics. One most conspicuously displayed, was that of relic gathering. Before the altar—which had been rudely

improvised—had been consecrated, these seekers for keepsakes of the occasion, commenced a regular onslaught upon the stones composing it, and vast
quantities were pocketed and carried off. All seemed to consider it a rare
occurrence, such as was never known in this country, if in the world, and
doubtless Frederick will be called upon to carve many a keystone out of the
granite which was embodied in the rough ashlars of the rude altar harshly
constructed on the top of the mountain and yesterday consecrated to the
mystic art.

It was very noticeable yesterday on the mountain, that some of the gazers
at the beautiful scenery were not content with the grandeur opened up by the
aid of telescopes and double-barrel eye-helpers, and were now and then look-
ing through the bottoms of tumblers, bottles and the like, with the most profound satisfaction.

AN INTERESTING EVENT.

A notable event in the Masonic history of Nevada—we may say in the
United States—occurred near the city yesterday. After the destruction of
their hall by fire, the Masons met for some time in the Lodge-room of the Odd
Fellows in the Odd Fellows' Building. This was likewise destroyed by fire a
few days ago, leaving the Order without an appropriate place of meeting. In
this emergency the Master of "Virginia Lodge, No. 3," in imitation of a custom of the Craft in ancient times, called a meeting of his Lodge on the summit of Mount Davidson yesterday afternoon. Over three hundred members
of the Order were in attendance. When it is considered that the top of
Mount Davidson is seven thousand eight hundred and twenty-seven feet above
the level of the sea, and nearly seventeen hundred feet above Virginia City,
the significance of this large convocation will be appreciated. The summit
of the mountain is a pointed mass of broken granite, yet almost upon the very
apex a rude altar was erected, and around it gathered over three
hundred Masons, who, in the heat of the mid-day sun, had toiled up the rug-
ged mountain side to witness the opening of a Masonic Lodge at a place so
unusual; and there, overlooking a city of twenty thousand people, the lodge
was opened partially in form, and its regular business transacted. From the
summit of the mountain, the country for a radius of perhaps a hundred miles
on every side is visible, with its towns, lakes, mountains, valleys, hoisting-
works, quartz-mills and railroads. This view is one of the grandest in the
State, and the gathering yesterday was in the eye of every Mason present,
scarcely less grand than the surroundings.

As the lodge was opened, the white emblem of the Order was thrown to
the breeze from the flag-staff on the summit, and the cheers that greeted it
must have been heard in the valleys below. Music, speeches and a bountiful
repast for all, enlivened the proceedings, and at five o'clock, or a few minutes
earlier, the concourse wended their way down the mountain side. Members
of the Order were in attendance from Gold Hill, Silver City, Dayton and
Carson, and so impressed were all present with the grandeur and solemnity
of the occasion, that the rude altar was almost chipped in pieces, to be preserved as mementoes of an event so unusual in the annals of the Order. It
is probable that a Mason's Lodge was never before opened in the United
States at so great an elevation—certainly never upon so prominent a point in
the light of day. The occasion will long be remembered, not only by those
present, but by the people of Storey County. In our local columns will be
seen a detailed account of what occurred, together with a full list of the members of the Order present.

NOTE.—As the compiler of this work was an active participant in the above event
and desirous that its record shall be preserved in book form, he has here inserted it
for the benefit of all whose names are therein enrolled as being present, as well as a
matter of great interest to the Craft in general. At that time he was the City Surveyor of Gold Hill, as well as a United States Deputy Surveyor and a member of Silver
Star Lodge, No. 5, at Gold Hill, at that time. He, with the assistance of Bro. Geo. W.

Dorwin, (now of Melrose, California,) surveyed the Sacred Square, in which the lodge was held and consecrated the altar with the corn, the wine and the oil, which he took up with him.

The full account as it appeared in the *Territorial Enterprise*, was printed on paper handkerchiefs, satin, silk and linen, by the thousands at the time, exhausting the dry good stores, whose merchant owners had to send to San Francisco to get fresh supplies. These uniquely printed copies were sent to Grand Lodges throughout the world and even to the Lodge at Jerusalem and thousands of other Lodges and Masons besides. The silk handkerchiefs upon which the account appeared, are treasured as mementoes, some of which are framed and adorn the halls and homes of the Brethren to which they have been dispersed.

Past Grand Masters J. C. Currie and Geo. W. Hopkins have crossed over to the other side of the Dark River, and the majority of those now living, who then participated, are residing in California, among them, Past Grand Master Robert W. Bollen, at Elsinore, in San Diego County, Past Deputy Grand Master Richard T. Mullard, at Los Angeles, and Past Grand Secretary R. H. Taylor, the Poet of the occasion, at San Francisco, engaged in the practice of the law. The memory of that interesting event will live until the last survivor of those there present shall have been called to eternal refreshment in that Grand Lodge above; but Mount Davidson will be known among the Craft as the "Mountain of the Lord," and the grandest altar of Freemasonry built by the Supreme Architect of the Universe himself, its solid base girdled with bands of gold and silver, and sparkling with its gems of crystal quartz, its altar cloth in winter, the purest snowy mantle spread over it by heaven itself, while the blazing sun, the silvery moon and the glittering stars shall be its greater and lesser lights to shine upon it, as long as the earth shall be used as a trestle-board by the Craft.

The Ancient Charges of a Freemason.

Extracted from the Ancient Records of Lodges beyond sea
and of those in England, Scotland and Ireland, for
the use of the Lodges in London. To be
read at the making of New Brethren, or when the Master shall
order it.*

THE GENERAL HEADS, viz:—

I.   Of God and Religion.
II. Of the Civil Magistrate, Supreme and Subordinate.
III. Of Lodges.
IV. Of Masters, Wardens, Fellows and Apprentices.
V.   Of the management of the Craft in working.
VI. Of Behavior, viz:—

1. In the Lodge while Constituted.
2. After the Lodge is over and the Brethren not gone.
3. When Brethren meet without Strangers, but not in a Lodge.
4. In presence of Strangers not Masons.
5. At Home and in the Neighborhood.
6. Toward a Strange Brother.

I. CONCERNING GOD AND RELIGION.

A Mason is obliged by his tenure, to obey the moral law; and if he rightly understands the art he will never be a stupid atheist nor an irreligious libertine. But though in ancient times Masons were charged in every country to be of the religion of that country or nation, whatever it was, it it now thought more expedient only to oblige them to that religion in which all men agree, leaving their particular opinions to themselves; that is, to be *good men and true*, or men of honor and honesty, by whatever denominations or persuasions they may be distinguished; whereby Masonry becomes the *center of union*, and the means of conciliating true friendship among persons that must have remained at a perpetual distance.

II. OF THE CIVIL MAGISTRATE, SUPREME AND SUBORDINATE.

A Mason is a peaceable subject to the civil powers wherever he resides or works, and is never to be concerned in plots and conspiracies against the peace and welfare of the nation, nor to behave himself undutifully to inferior magistrates; for as Masonry hath always been injured by war, bloodshed and confusion, so ancient kings and princes have been much disposed to encourage the craftsmen, because of their peaceableness and loyalty, whereby they practically answered the cavils of their adversaries, and promoted the honor of the Fraternity, who ever flourished in times of peace. So that if a brother should

*These charges were prepared and presented to the Grand Lodge of England in 1721 by Dr. Anderson and Dr. Desaguliers, and having been approved by the Grand Lodge on the 25th of March, 1722, were published in the first edition of the Book of Constitutions. They have always been held in the highest veneration by the Fraternity, as embodying the most important points of the ancient *written*, as well as unwritten law of Masonry.

be a rebel against the State, he is not to be countenanced in his rebellion, however he may be pitied as an unhappy man; and if convicted of no other crime, though the loyal Brotherhood must and ought to disown his rebellion, and give no umbrage or ground of political jealousy to the government for the time being, they cannot expel him from the Lodge, and his relation to it remains indefeasible.

III. OF LODGES.

A Lodge is a place where Masons assemble and work; hence that assembly, or duly organized society of Masons, is called a *Lodge*, and every Brother ought to belong to one, and to be subject to its By-laws and the General Regulations. It is either particular or general, and will be best understood by attending it, and by the Regulations of the General or Grand Lodge hereunto annexed. In ancient times no Master or Fellow could be absent from it, especially when warned to appear at it, without incurring a s vere censure, until it appeared to the Master and wardens that pure necessity hindered him.

The persons admitted members of a Lodge must be good and true men, free-born, and of mature and discreet age, no bond-men, no women, no immoral or scandalous men, but of good report.

IV. OF MASTERS, WARDENS, FELLOWS AND APPRENTICES.

All preferment among Masons is grounded upon real worth and personal merit only; that so the Lords may be well served, the Brethren not put to shame, nor the Royal Craft despised: Therefore no Master or Warden is chosen by seniority, but for his merit. It is impossible to describe these things in writing, and every Brother must attend in his place, and learn them in a way peculiar to this Fraternity. Only candidates may know that no Master should take an Apprentice unless he has sufficient employment for him, and unless he be a perfect youth, having no maim or defect in his body, that may render him uncapable of learning the art of serving his Master's Lord, and of being made a *Brother*, and then a *Fellow Craft* in due time, even after he has served such a term of years as the custom of the country directs; and that he should be descended of honest parents; that so, when otherwise qualified, he may arrive at the honor of being the *Warden*, and then the *Master* of the Lodge, the *Grand Warden*, and at length the *Grand Master* of all Lodges, according to his merit.

No Brother can be a Warden until he has passed the part of a Fellow Craft; nor a Master until he has acted as a Warden, nor Grand Warden until he has been Master of a Lodge, nor GRAND MASTER unless he has been a Fellow Craft before his election, who is also to be nobly born, or a gentleman of the best fashion, or some eminent scholar, or some curious architect, or other artist, descended of honest parents, and who is of singular great merit in the opinion of the Lodges. And for the better, and easier, and more honorable discharge of his office, the Grand Master has a power to choose his own Deputy Grand Master, who must be then, or must have been formerly, the Master of a particular Lodge, and has the privilege of acting whatever the Grand Master, his principal, should act, unless the said principal be present or interpose his authoity by a letter. ·

These rulers and governors, supreme and subordinate, of the ancient Lodge, are to be obeyed in their respective stations by all the Brethren, according to Old Charges and regulations, with all humility, reverence, love and alactrity.

V. OF THE MANAGEMENT OF THE CRAFT IN WORKING.

All Masons shall work honestly on working day, that they may live creditably on holy days; and the time appointed by the law of the land, or confirmed by custom, shall be observed.

The most expert of the Fellow Craftsmen shall be appointed or chosen the Master or Overseer of the Lord's work; who is to be called *Master* by those that work under him. The Craftsmen are to avoid all ill language, and to call each other by no disobliging name, but Brother or Fellow; and to behave themselves courteously within and without the Lodge.

The Master knowing himself to be able of cunning, shall undertake the Lord's work as reasonably as possible, and truly dispend his goods as if they were his own; nor to give more wages to any Brother or Apprentice than he really may deserve.

Both the Master and the Masons receiving their wages justly, shall be faithful to the Lord, and honestly finish their work, whether task or journey; nor put the work to task that hath been accustomed to journey.

None shall discover envy at the prosperity of a Brother, nor supplant him, or put him out of his work, if he be capable to finish the same; for no man can finish another's work so much to the Lord's profit, unless he be thoroughly acquainted with the designs and draughts of him that begun it.

When a Fellow Craftsman is chosen Warden of the work under the Master, he shall be true both to Master and Fellows, shall carefully oversee the work in the Master's absence to the Lord's profit; and his Brethren shall obey him.

All Masons employed shall meekly receive their wages without murmuring or mutiny, and not desert the Master until the work is finished.

A younger Brother shall be instructed in working, to prevent spoiling the materials for want of judgment, and for increasing and continuing of brotherly love.

All the tools in working shall be approved by the Grand Lodge.

No laborer shall be employed in the proper work of Masonry; nor shall Freemasons work with those that are not free, without an urgent necessity; nor shall they teach laborers and unaccepted Masons as they should teach a Brother or Fellow.

VI. OF BEHAVIOR, viz:

1. IN THE LODGE WHILE CONSTITUTED.

You are not to hold private committees, or separate conversation, without leave from the Master, nor to talk of anything impertinent or unseemly, nor interrupt the Master or Wardens, or any Brother speaking to the Master; nor behave yourself ludicrously or jestingly while the Lodge is engaged in what is serious and solemn; nor use any unbecoming language upon any pretence whatsoever; but to pay due reverence to your Master, Wardens and Fellows, and put them to worship.

If any complaint be brought, the Brother found guilty shall stand to the award and determination of the Lodge, who are the proper and competent judges of all such controversies (unless you carry it by appeal to the Grand Lodge) and to whom they ought to be referred, unless a Lord's work be hindered the meanwhile, in which case a particular reference may be made; but you must never go to law about what concerns *Masonry*, without an absolute necessity apparent to the Lodge.

2. BEHAVIOR AFTER THE LODGE IS OVER AND THE BRETHREN NOT GONE.

You may enjoy yourself with innocent mirth, treating one another according to ability, but avoiding all excess, or forcing any Brother to eat or drink beyond his inclination, or hindering him from going when his occasions call him, or doing or saying anything offensive, or that may forbid an *easy* and *free* conversation; for that would blast our harmony and defeat our laudable purposes. Therefore no private piques or quarrels must be brought within the door of the Lodge, far less quarrels about religion, or nations or state policy we being only as Masons of the Catholic (universal) religion above mentioned; we are also of all nations, tongues, kindreds, and languages, and are resolved against *all politics*, as what never yet conduced to the welfare of the Lodge, nor ever will. *This* CHARGE *has always been strictly enjoined and observed*; BUT ESPECIALLY EVER SINCE THE REFORMATION IN BRITAIN, OR THE DISSENT AND SECESSION OF THESE NATIONS FROM THE COMMUNION OF ROME.

3. BEHAVIOR WHEN BRETHREN MEET WITHOUT STRANGERS, BUT NOT IN A LODGE FORMED.

You are to salute one another in a courteous manner, as you will be instructed, calling each other *Brother*, freely giving mutual instruction as shall be thought expedient, without being overseen or overheard, and without encroaching upon each other, or derogating from that respect which is due to any Brother, were he not a Mason; for though all Masons are as brethren upon the same level, yet Masonry takes no honor from a man that he had before; nay, rather it adds to his honor, especially if he has deserved well of the Brotherhood, who must give honor to whom it is due, and avoid ill manners.

4. BEHAVIOR IN PRESENCE OF STRANGERS NOT MASONS.

You shall be cautious in your words and carriage, that the most penetrating stranger shall not be able to discover or find out what is not proper to be intimated; and sometimes you shall divert a discourse, and manage it prudently for the honor of the Worshipful Fraternity.

5. BEHAVIOR AT HOME, AND IN YOUR NEIGHBORHOOD.

You are to act as becomes a moral and wise man; particularly, not to let your family, friends and neighbors know the concerns of the Lodge, etc., but wisely to consult your own honor, and that of the Ancient Brotherhood, for reasons not to be mentioned here. You must also consult your health by not continuing together too late, or too long from home, after Lodge hours are past; and by avoiding of gluttony or drunkenness, that your families be not neglected or injured, nor you disabled from working.

6. BEHAVIOR TOWARD A STRANGE BROTHER.

You are cautiously to examine him, in such a method as prudence shall direct you, that you may not be imposed upon by an ignorant, false pretender, whom you are to reject with contempt and derision, and beware of giving any hints of knowledge.

But if you discover him to be a true and genuine Brother, you are to respect him accordingly, and if he is in want, you must relieve him if you can, or else direct him how he may be relieved; you must employ him some days, or else recommend him to be employed.   But you are not charged to do beyond your ability, only to prefer a poor Brother, that is a good man and true, before any other poor people in the same circumstances.

Finally, All these CHARGES you are to observe, and also those that shall be communicated to you in another way; cultivating brotherly love, the foundation and cap-stone, the cement and glory of this Ancient Fraternity, avoiding all wrangling and quarreling, all slander and backbiting, nor permitting others to slander any other Brother, but defending his character, and doing him all good offices, as far as is consistent with your honor and safety and no further.   And if any of them do you injury, you must apply to your own or his Lodge; and from thence you may appeal to the Grand Lodge at the Quarterly Communication, and from thence to the Annual Grand Lodge, as has been the ancient laudable conduct of our forefathers in every nation; never taking a legal course, but when the case cannot be otherwise decided, and patiently listening to the honest and friendly advice of Master and Fellows when they would prevent you going to law with strangers, or would excite you to put a speedy period to all law-suits, that so you may mind the affair of Masonry with the more alacrity and success; but with respect to Brothers or Fellows at law, the Master and Brethren should kindly offer their mediation, which ought to be thankfully submitted to by the contending Brethren; and if that submission is impracticable, they must, however, carry on their process or lawsuit without wrath and rancor, (not in the common way) saying or doing nothing that may hinder brotherly love, and good offices to be renewed and continued; that all may see the benign influence of Masonry, as all true Masons have done from the beginning of the world, and will do to the end of time.   Amen.   So mote it be.